PRE-COLONIAL INDIA AND THE WEST

INDIA IN THE EYES OF PRE-COLONIAL TRAVELERS FROM THE WEST

Zacharias P. Thundy

Northern Michigan University

Thoma Books

CONTENTS

Introduction

Early Period

1. India and the Old Testament
2. The Greeks and India
A. Before Alexander
B. Alexander
C. After Alexander
D. Non-Christian Travelers
E. Christian Witnesses
India's Debt to the Greeks

Medieval Period (AD 500–1500)

1. Pilgrims and Travelers (AD 500-800)
2. Religion and Travel (AD 800-1500)
A. Benjamin of Tudela
B. Marco Polo
C. Indian Erotic Art in Marco Polo's Eyes
3. Christian Missionaries
A. John of Monte Corvino
B. Friar Odoric
C. Friar Jordanus
D. John de Marignoli
E. India in Medieval Imagination

India in the Age of "Discovery": Decline and the
    Demise of a Myth

Shakespeare's Dissenting Voice in *The Tempest*
  Against Colonial Misperceptions.

Conclusion

Works Cited

Notes on "Divine" Caliban

Final Conclusion

NOTES

Thundy

BOOKS WRITTEN OR EDITED BY THE AUTHOR*, SOME OF WHICH WERE PUBLISHED UNDER THE PSEUDONYM "JANUS RASMUS" (AMAZON)

1. *Covenant in Anglo-Saxon Thought.*

2. *Chaucerian Problems and Perspectives*

3. *Buddha and Christ: Nativity Stories and Indian Traditions.*

4. *Religions in Dialogue: East and West Meet.*

5. *Millennium: Apocalypse, Antichrist, and Old English Monsters c. 1000.*

6. *Trial of Jesus and His Death on the Cross: Buddhist Sources of   Gospel Narratives.*

7. *Language and Culture: A Book of Readings.*

8. *In Geardagum (In Days of Yore): Beowulf, Apocalypse and the East.*

9. *Rabbouni (John 21:16) by Mary Magdalene: A Misreading.*

10. *Gospels and Greek Classics.*

11. *Is Notre Dame Still A Catholic University?:*

12. *God: A Short Study in Etymology.*

13. *Pre-Colonial India and the West: India in the Eyes of Pre-Colonial Travelers from the West.*

14. *The Stupa and the Cross: Gospel Narratives of the Passion and Death of Jesus and Their Buddhist Sources.*

15. *Holy Mary Magdalene: Old and New.*

16. *Catholic Church's Marriage Dilemmas.*

17. *Divorce, Remarriage and the Eucharist.*

18. *J' Accuse: Catholic Church's Continuing Persecution of Gays and condemnation of Same-Sex Marriage.*

19. *Who Am I to Judge?*

20. *Jesus in Egypt.*

21. *Jesus Was Also Pro-Choice?: Bible and Abortion.*

22. *Letter vs. Spirit.*

23. *Personhood of the Embryo.*

24. *Moral Dimensions of Abortion and Contraception.*

25. *The South Indian Folklore of the Kadar.*

26. *Papers in Linguistics.*

27. *Dialect Survey of the Upper Peninsula of*

Michigan.

28. *Stories from the East and the West.*

29. *English Poetry: An Introduction.*

30. *Kerala: People and Culture.*

31. *Modern Malayalam Literature: An Anthology. 2 vols.*

32. *Hamlet's "Too Too Solid Flesh" and "The Dram of Eale": Heart of the Matter.*

* The author, an alumnus of the University of Notre Dame and a retired professor at Northern Michigan University, holds three advanced degrees in philosophy, religion, and literature from three distinguished universities. He is a linguist, anthropologist, philosopher, theologian, and literary critic or, in short, a dabbling renaissance man but never a perfectionist.

Introduction

During the early days of the Indian War of Independence, alias the "Indian Mutiny" of May 1857), reports of systematic rape and dismemberment of British women by "savage" Indians circulated in British India and England. British magistrates who examined accusers and eyewitnesses could not find evidence of systematic rape and mutilation. But such rumors of atrocities associated with the "Mutiny" continued to haunt the imagination of British novelists who wrote about India subsequently, as in E. M. Forster, *A Passage to India* and in Paul Scott, *The Jewel in the Crown.*[1] What is remarkable about this phenomenon is that after the "Mutiny" the noble Indian in the imagination of the Greeks was transformed into a barbarian capable of rape--a changed view found earlier in Shakespeare's *Tempest*[2]. Christopher Columbus also had a similar change of mind: in his first encounter with the Native Americans, Columbus the explorer at first found them unspoiled, kind, and gentle, much like the pre-lapsarian Adam and Eve[3], but during his second stay in Hispaniola as a colonial power broker he appeared to have accepted the testimony of men like Diego Alvarez Chanca that the Carib Indians were ferocious cannibals. He refused to recognize their right of self-determination and kidnapped Indian men and women to serve as guides or interpreters. In December 1492, he placed upon the Indians heavy demands of tribute and gave many as slaves to the Spanish colonists, creating in Admiral Morison's words "hell in Hispaniola."[4] The garrison he had set up in Haiti--La Navidad--was destroyed, and the soldiers were killed by natives outraged at the rapes and thefts of the Spanish who left the garrison to collect gold. Columbus soon ordered beheadings, and before too long the Tainos were extinct. In Columbus's mind reports of the existence of cannibalism in the Caribbean only confirmed the stories told by classical and medieval writers of anthropophagi in the extreme Orient--Columbus thought he was getting closer to India, his goal.[5] It took only a few years for the image of the Native American to undergo a change, from sublime to savage, in Western perception during the late fifteenth and early sixteenth centuries. About the same time the image of India also underwent a similar radical change in Western imagination, the difference being that it took about two millennia for the latter change to take place, which is the thesis of this article. This study will also refer to the causes that brought about this change in the Western perception of India.

Though the emphasis of this study is on medieval European travelers and their impressions of India, the medieval reporters' place in travel literature can be understood only in terms of the writings of earlier European travel reporters on whom the medieval travelers relied for information and guidance. Likewise, the contributions of the medieval travelers have to be appreciated in the light of the written records left by the early modern travelers who, following the lead of their immediate predecessors, mounted organized maritime expeditions to India in search of gold and spices. Indeed, as the twelfth-century philosopher Bernardus Silvestris, and later Isaac Newton, has observed, we are like dwarves standing on the shoulders of giants. Therefore, on account of this continuity between giants and dwarves, between ancients and moderns, this quest for meaning behind Western travels to India must also begin with classical antiquity and end in the age of discovery, which is also our own modern age.[6] Needless to add that my "ambitious" panoramic enterprise, which covers a span of some two thousand years in the space of a little book has to be highly selective of its source materials by "freezing the moments" or by selecting the pregnant moments in history as in photographs or sculptures.

EARLY PERIOD (600 BC - AD 500)

Most people travel to other countries to do business or to explore opportunities to study, preach, immigrate, colonize, and/or visit as tourists. While today most travelers are either business people and tourists, in early times they were, with the exception of a few, primarily merchants who sold their wares in India and carried back with them reports, rumors, and Indian goods about. Tidbits from their often exaggerated travelogues were included in treatises about India in the works written not only in the Greco-Roman world but also in the Hebrew Bible and the Christian Bible.

In the European imagination of antiquity, "Asia," "East," and "India" were imprecise. Before the age of the great discoveries, these terms were used so interchangeably that Egypt was sometimes pictured in maps as situated in Asia, which stood as a synonym for India.[7] Sometimes Parthia included India as well. This means that when the Gospel of Matthew speaks about the magi from the East, it is possible that he means India; so also when the Acts of the

Apostles describes the nationalities of the God-fearing Jews who were in Jerusalem for the Pentecost, he probably includes Indians among the people from Asia and Parthia (Acts 2:9-10). In spite of their lack of scientific knowledge of India, educated people in antiquity knew a great deal about the land and its people.

1. India and the Old Testament

India is mentioned in Esther 1:1 and 8:9 as the eastern boundary of the Persian Empire under Ahasuerus (c. fifth century BC.) and in 1 Maccabees 6:37 in a reference to the Indian mahouts of Antiochus's war elephants (second century BC.). Otherwise there are no explicit references to India in the Old Testament. However, archeological evidences of the Kulli culture of Baluchistan indicate that from c. 2800 BC., there were contacts between Mesopotamia (the home of the eponymous ancestor of the Jewish people) and the great cities of the Indus civilization.[8] At the sites of ancient Sumerian cities of Kish, Lagash, and Ur, archeologists have discovered typical objects of the Indus civilization that indicate there existed a flourishing trade in spices between India and Mesopotamia. The presence of Indian ivory objects of foreign workmanship discovered in Mesopotamia suggests that they were imported from India. Since commerce by its nature is mutual, it is probable that the cultural interaction was mutual between these geographical regions.

There are some indirect references to India in the Old Testament. According to 1 Kings 9:26-28, King Solomon's navy (c. 1000 BC.), sailed to Ophir to fetch gold. Since Ophir is *Sopheir/Sophara* in the LXX, since *Sophir* means India in Coptic, and since gold was plentiful in the mountains north of Punjab in Northwest India, it is generally accepted that Ophir was a port in India. Sedlar writes:

> In favor of Ophir as India are the facts that the geographer Ptolemaios (Ptolemy) notes an "Abiria" (Ophir?) at the mouth of the Indus, that Buddhist writings refer to the coast around Bombay as "Sovira" (possibly Ptolemaios' "Supara"), and that the Jewish historian Josephos (first century. AD.) identifies the Biblical "Sopheir" with the Indian "Land of Gold."[9]

Certain other Indian products, such as ivory, the peacock, and the monkey going to King Solomon's court suggests that they must have originated in India. I Kings 10:22 explicitly states that every third year King Solomon's navy, together with King Hiram's, brought him "gold, silver, ivory, apes, and peacocks." The Old Testament words for peacock *tuki,* for ivory *shen habbim,* and for the ape *kof* all seem to be derived from their Indian counterparts *tokei, ab,* and *kapi* respectively. [10] Indian textiles and fragrances also seem to have made their way to the world of the Old Testament: Proverbs 7:17, Ps. 45:8, and Song of Solomon 4:14 refer to the Indian fragrant wood called aloes (Heb. *ahalim* by a term derived from Sanskrit *agaru* and from cognates in Tamil and Malayalam; the Greek *sandalon* is a derivative of the Sanskrit/Malayalam *chandana* ;[11] ancient Babylonian texts refer to linen as *sindhu* (*sindon* in Greek, meaning "Indian"); Isaiah 3:23 refers to *sadin* for fine linen.[12] Rice was brought to European ports from South India; the word *rice* is a shortened form of the Spanish *arroz,* derived from the Arabic *aruz*; the Greek *oruza* and the Latin *oryza* are perhaps derived from Arabic or from the Tamil *arisi.*[13] As Sedlar argues, "the juxtaposition of three or four products known to be found in India, together with the sailing of Solomon's ships to "Ophir," lends weight to the supposition that sea-commerce with India already was in existence."[14] It may be added that the Greek word *drachma,* which is found in many vernacular languages, is derived from the Prakrit *dramma* and the modern *dam,* which survives in the modern English expression, "I don't give a *damn*."

Not only part of King Solomon's wealth but also some of his wisdom seems to have been derived from India. For instances, some passages in chapter 30 of the book of Proverbs attributed to Solomon are derived from the *Rgveda*, *Panchatantra*, and *Hitopadesa*; likewise, the famous judgment of the legendary king.(1 Kings 3: 16-28) from Jataka 546; the same Mahosadha Jataka Tale also yields the story of Susanna found in Daniel 13: 1-64. The Jewish people came in contact with Indian stories most likely during their captivity in Babylon in the sixth century BC. Incidentally, Jataka 339 speaks of a voyage from India to Baveru (Bavli/Babylon).[15] The upshot of these observations is simply that the Hebrews seem to have regarded India with respect, as the legendary source of material wealth and proverbial wisdom.

2. The Greeks and India

A. Before Alexander

It is a fact that many Greeks give the Orientals at least some credit for the contributions they have made to Greek thought and ideals. Zeller writes: "The Greeks themselves were inclined from early times...to grant the peoples of the Orient, the only ones whose intellectual culture preceded their own that they had a share in the origination of their philosophy. In the early days it is only individual doctrines which in this manner are derived from the Orient."[16]

This Greek recognition of Oriental contribution should be seen as a sign of the classical Greek's readiness to learn from alien sources; the Greek word *historia* implies curiosity, openness for the alien, the other, and journeys outside Greece since Greek philosophers and historians were supposed to have traveled to foreign countries in search of wisdom.[17] The earliest recorded use of the word "philosophize" occurs in the context of travel for the sake of theory.[18] Pythagoras, the alleged inventor of the word "philosophy," is reported to have traveled widely and to have been the recipient and transmitter of Oriental wisdom.[19] Herodotus, Plato, and Aristotle also emphasize the Greek debt to the Orient while they equally stress the independence of Greek thought. Though Plato never mentions India in his writings, he himself is reported in later literature to have traveled to India.[20]

Though the Orient in the thought of the early Greek philosophers was primarily Egypt, the storehouse of ancient learning, the http://ndsmcobserver.com/geographers Scylax and Ctesias, who were in the service of Persian kings, brought Indian topography and mythology closer to Greece. For instance, Ctesias' "dog-headed" creatures correspond to the Sanskrit *Sunamukha* or *svamukha*, those with "blanket ears" are the Sanskrit *karnapravarana*, and the "one-footed" creature is the Sanskrit *ekapada*. [21] In Halbfass's assessment, "some ideas which later generations associated frequently and commonly with Indian religion and the Indian way of life, such as vegetarianism...and the contempt for death, already emerged in the pre-Alexandrian image of India."[22] What is, therefore, clear from the few references cited above is that the religion and philosophy of India had not yet played a major role in the development of Greek thought till the end of the fourth century BC.

B. Alexander

Alexander (356 - 323 BC.), who had learned something about Asia from his tutor Aristotle broke through the Persian defenses that separated the Greek world from India and waged a military campaign in northwest India. Alexander's conquest served as a watershed in the Greek understanding of Asia and brought the Indian subcontinent into direct communication with Greece. A court historian kept daily records of Alexander's campaign up to the year 327 BCE. The philosopher Callisthenes of Olynthus accompanied Alexander and wrote about his exploits till his departure from Bactria to India. Four factual histories of Alexander's campaigns were written after Alexander's death by eyewitnesses: by Nearchos the admiral, by Onesikritos the chief pilot, by Aristobolus the architect, and by Ptolemy the general and later founder of the famous Egyptian dynasty named for him. Besides being glorifications of Alexander, these accounts were also faithful reports about India. Though they are not available in their original versions, Arrian's *Indica* (c. 150 AD.) preserved much of the information contained in them. At least twenty of Alexander's contemporaries wrote histories about him.[23] The tendency of these historians was to portray Alexander along the existing literary parallels of the heroes of the Trojan War, which convention was a commonplace in the literature of the period. Facts were soon mixed up with fancy in the Alexander romances which became popular after the death of Alexander; Cleitarchus of Colophon and Pseudo-Callisthenes of Alexandria (c. AD. 200) composed such works that later fired the popular and literary imagination of the Middle Ages.[24]

Alexander conquered not merely to destroy and plunder, though, of course, he sought military glory in all his campaigns. Being the recipient of the best education of his time from Aristotle, he was an admirer of culture and literature. For him conquest was also a means for scientific discovery; that was the reason he included writers and scientists in his military campaigns.[25] Alexander really wanted to conciliate those whom he had conquered and attempted an amalgamation process in government, religion, military, and art. Accordingly, he sometimes wore Persian dress and adopted Persian imperial ceremonial at the Macedonian court; he appointed many non-Greeks to important positions in government administration; he ordered the teaching of the Greek language to native youths; above all, he promoted intermarriages between Persians and Greeks, himself setting the example by marrying the Persian princess Roxane. In many conquered territories he established Greek garrisons, which naturally served as the outposts of Hellenic civilization.[26] The natural outcome of this syncretist movement on the part of Alexander was that the mixed generation of later Greek rulers deliberately tried to fuse Greek and Oriental cultures: they erected buildings and planned towns in the Greek style and treated native deities as identical with Greek deities with similar features. This Hellenism sponsored by Alexander was characterized by syncretism, tolerance, cosmopolitanism, and openness to foreign ideas.[27]

C. After Alexander

Three major results of the Macedonian invasion and the Greek occupation of northwest India were the acquisition and dissemination of knowledge about India, the establishment of an influential hybrid Hellenistic civilization in Bactria, the Greeks' encounter with the Indian wise men, and the spread of Buddhism in central Asia.

The major source of the West's knowledge about India was Megasthenes. He could write with the authority of an eyewitness on the geography, climate, customs, and culture of the Indians. Later historians tended to accept everything Megasthenes said and continued to talk about the extreme temperatures of India, of its mighty rivers, of the absence of the Great Bear from the night sky, of the monsoons, and of the pearls collected in south India. Sugar cane, precious stones, cotton, spices, and drugs found in India made the Greeks consider India as a wealthy country. Wonderment about India grew apace with Megasthenes' description of the huge banyan trees, deadly snakes, man-like monkeys, and enormous elephants. Megasthenes also wrote about the bright-colored cotton clothes that people wore, the diet of rice and meat, and the absence of wine. He distinguished the fair-skinned Aryans of the north from the dark-hued southerners. Megasthenes talked about the "philosophers" as the smallest but the highest class among the seven groups of people he encountered in India. He observed the practice of polygamy, the fascinating ritual of sati (suttee), and many other customs and laws of the people, which constitute one of the valuable sources for the study of ancient law in India.[28]

Eratosthenes, the famous librarian at Alexandria from about 234-196 BC., collated all the available information about the topography of India and included it in his *Geographica*, a work which is lost now, but summarized by Strabo along with criticisms of it by Hipparchus.[29] Eratosthenes was the first writer to present India as a peninsula; he described Ganges as flowing eastward to the ocean, shortened the dimensions of both Ganges and Indus, and indicated the existence of the island Taprobane (Sri Lanka/Ceylon).[30]

Strabo (c. 63 BC b- AD. 21), the author of six historical books on Asia in Greek and a conserver of earlier geographers, reports that about this time the Ptolemies of Egypt sent Eudoxos of Kyzikos on a trade mission to India. In this expedition the Greeks had help from a shipwrecked Indian captain rescued from the Egyptian waters; they continued on their voyage to India and purchased precious stones and fragrances.[31] Strabo also gives information of a flourishing trade between

Egypt and India in the first century BC. during the Roman rule. He himself accompanied one such trade trip down the Nile to Ethiopia, where goods were transferred overland to Myos Hormos on the Red Sea. About this time Alexandrian merchants used to send about 120 ships to India.[32] Obviously, the *pax romana*, ushered in by Emperor Augustus (27 BC. - AD. 14), helped cut down the incidence of Arab piracy on the high seas and improve direct trade relations between India and the Roman empire.[33] It is to be mentioned in passing that Pomponius Mela, the first Latin geographer whose work has survived, has nothing significant to add to the West's knowledge of India.[34]

A first-century (AD.) work, the *Periplus of the Erithraean Sea* ("Circuit of the Indian Ocean"), an anonymous Greek work originally written in Egypt by a Roman subject around 50, gives clear, concise, and accurate information about Roman trade with India. The author talks about harbor facilities, political conditions, customs duties, and merchant wares in the different places along the trade route to India.[35] The writer, who uses first-person pronoun in parts of the book, may have traveled with the merchants on a trip to India. At the port of Barygaza, the author says, the Greeks traded wine, copper, tin, lead, coral, topaz, gold, silver, sweet clover, and other items which were exchanged for a profit with the money of the country. The king of the land purchased from the Greeks silver vessels, singing boys, beautiful maidens for his harem, fine wines, and thin clothing. In his description of Muziris, he says that the port city abounds in ships sent there with cargoes from Arabia and with the boats of the Greeks.[36] A fourth-century map known as the Peutinger Table shows a temple dedicated to divine Augustus at the mouth of River Kaveri, which suggests that there were Romans living there in the first century BC.[37]

Linguistics and literature supply some supporting evidence to Greek trade with India. As mentioned before, many Greek words for Indian products, such as those for cinnamon, ginger, cloves, rice, brown sugar, camphor, nard, apes, sapphire, emerald, opal, lapis lazuli, and sandalwood, have corresponding cognate words in Tamil, Malayalam, and/or Sanskrit.[38] The Tamil epic of *Cilappadikaram* refers to Greek ships which brought gold to Muziris and left laden with pepper, to Greek mansions at the mouth of Kaveri river, to the Greek carpenters who built a palace for the Tamil king, and to Greek bodyguards in the service of the Tamil king.[39]

Archeological evidence also indicates that the Greeks and Romans engaged in significant trade with south India. One typical site that has yielded much evidence for Western trade activity in the first century was the port of "Poudouke" (modern Pondicherry) mentioned by *Periplus* and the Ptolemy.[40] Sedlar writes:

> Poudouke by the middle of the first century CE. was a brick-built emporium with extensive storage and manufacturing facilities. To this port came Indian ships carrying precious stones from Ceylon, silks and spices from the Ganges region. Greek merchants arriving overland from the Malabar coast met them there. Fairly superficial digging at the site of Poudouke has unearthed enormous quantities of Western material, indicative of the large volume of commerce conducted at this place. Articles of Mediterranean origin-- most notably the Italian red-glazed "Arretine" pottery, which went out of production about 45 AD.--are here suddenly super-imposed upon a purely native and local culture. The excavations

at Poudouke provide striking confirmation of the older literary evidence that the reign of Augustus at Rome witnessed a significant upsurge in the Indo-Mediterranean trade.[41]

Hoards of Roman coins have been excavated in different parts of south India, especially those from the period of Augustus to Nero. Just recently, archeologists excavating around the South Indian state of Andhra Pradesh have unearthed more than 15,000 Roman gold and silver coins bearing the impressions of the Roman emperors Augustus, Tiberius, Nero, and Plotina, the wife of Trajan. The most rewarding single dig was at Akkenapalli in Nalgonda district, where more than 1,000 Roman gold and silver coins were unearthed.[42] It seems that Indian kings and merchants considered the Roman coins primarily as gold and silver bullions and as capital reserves rather than as a means of exchange since these coin hoards also had jewelry and other valuables and since much of the trade was in the nature of barter.

The increased trade between Rome and India in the first century resulted in a huge trade deficit for Rome with the outflow o gold and silver from the empire. This situation caused some serious concern for the Roman economists. According to Pliny, who wrote during Vespasian's reign (69-79 AD.), "the maritime commerce between India and the Roman empire caused the export of over 50 million sesterces ($ 5,000,000) annually to India, or 100 million sesterces ($10,000,000) for India, China, and the Arabian Peninsula taken together."[43] Emperor Tiberius complained to the Roman senate in a letter about this financial drain due to the purchase of female slaves and luxury items like Kashmir wool, ivory, pearls, tortoise shell, silk, and precious stones.[44] Pliny lamented: "This is the sum which our luxuries and our women cost us."[45]

D. Non-Christian Travelers

The third-century sophist Philostratos gives a long description of Apollonius of Tyana's first-century travels in India. According to Philostratos, Apollonius traveled widely and visited India, where he spent four months and was instructed in the wisdom of the Brahmins. Apollonius' travel purpose was the attainment of wisdom. He said to the Brahmins: "I consider that your lore is profounder and much more divine than our own," and he asked that he be taught: "Will you teach me then...all this wisdom?"[46] The Indian king Phraotes wrote to Iarchus, his Indian master, a letter in Greek regarding the intentions of Apollonius: "Apollonius, wisest of men, yet accounts you still wiser than himself, and is come to learn your lore. Send him away therefore when he knows all that you know yourselves, assured that nothing of your teachings will perish, for in discourse and memory he excels all men."[47] Apollonius himself acknowledged his gratitude to his Indian hosts in the letter he wrote to Iarchus as he left India:

I came to you on foot, and yet you presented me with the sea; but by sharing with me the wisdom which is yours, you have made it mine even to travel through the heavens. All this I shall mention to the Hellenes; and I shall communicate in my words with them as if you were present, unless I have in vain drunk the draught of Tantalus. Farewell, ye goodly philosophers.[48]

Apollonius lived like the ascetics of India, professing his belief metempsychosis and practicing vegetarianism, and claiming that the Pythagorean way of life had come from India via Egypt.[49] In a conversation with the future emperor Vespasian, he said that he followed the religion of the Indians.[50]

What is to be inferred from this is not that everything Philostratos says about Apollonius is true, but that Philostratos had genuine information about India and that Apollonius of the first century also knew and admired India. According to the testimony of Lucian of Samasota, in the middle of the second century AD., Demetrius, the Greek philosopher, also went to India and settled down among the Brahmins.[51]

Philo (d. AD. 50), mentioned above, also knew about the Indian gymnosophists and admired their natural philosophy; he thought they deserved as much praise as Abraham.[52] Apuleius (AD. 160-170) also was favorably impressed the customs and aspirations of the gymnosophists.[53] Plutarch had reservations in his approval of the gymnosophists' way of life, partly due to his Orientalism.[54]

It is quite likely that the Neo-Platonists of Alexandria also could have come under the influence of Indian thought. Plotinus (203-270), the outstanding exponent of this philosophy, was such an admirer of Indian wisdom that, in an effort to learn from the magi of Persia and the Brahmins of India, he attached himself to the Roman emperor Gordianus III who was then marching with his army to Asia. Plotinus did not reach India, but barely escaped with life when Gordianus was murdered in Mesopotamia.[55] Plotinus must have had some knowledge about Indian philosophy; otherwise he would not have embarked for India. Probably Plotinus, who spent most of his life in Alexandria, learned it from books available at the famous Alexandrian library or from Indians who lived in Alexandria or from his master Ammonius Sakkas, whose disciple he was for eleven years.[56]

Ammonius, according to Eusebius, was a Christian who turned pagan. Perhaps the clue to his paganism can be gleaned from his sobriquet--"Sakkas"--which corresponds to no other Greek word. As Eric Segelberg has argued, the word cannot mean "sack wearer," or any other known Greek word; he thinks that "Sakkas" is a variation of the Indian word "Sakya," the tribal name of Buddha the Sakya

Muni whose followers are known by the phrase "sons of the Sakya."[57] It is quite possible that Ammonius was a Greek Buddhist! Ammonius was also the teacher of the Origen, whose writings also show affinities to Indian thought.[58] There is, however, one dissenting voice, which rejects the Oriental origins of Greek wisdom, among the Greeks. It is that of the third-century (A.D.) Greek doxographer Diogenes Laërtius, who tries to refute the thesis that philosophy had its origin among barbarians like the Persians, Chaldeans, Egyptians, and Indians. [59]

E. Christian Witnesses

There should be some truth in the Christian legends about the visits of Thomas and Bartholomew, the Apostles of Jesus, to India. These men could have travelled to India in the company of merchants either by land or by boat.

The Indian account of the St. Thomas Christians of the Malabar coast says that Thomas landed at Kodungalloor (Cranganore) in 52 A.D., converted twelve Brahmin families to Christianity, founded seven churches on the west coast, and then died the death of martyr at Mylapore, near Madras, on the east coast. These Indian traditions are found in the third-century *Acts of Judas Thomas,* probably composed at Edessa. The story of Thomas is as follows:

After the death of Jesus, the disciples divided up the world for evangelization by casting lots; India fell to Thomas' lot. Thomas was not happy about this assignment. Meanwhile Jesus sold Thomas as a slave to the merchant Habban who was going to India. The merchant and the Apostle travelled together to the capital of King Gundaphar, who asked Thomas to build a royal palace and advanced him large sums of money. Thomas spent all the money on the poor. When called to account for the money, Thomas said that he had already built the royal palace, not on earth, but in heaven. The incredulous king threw Thomas in prison. About this time, the king's brother died and appeared in a dream to the king and showed him the palace that Thomas built for him in heaven. The repentant king released Thomas from prison and accepted Christianity. Later, Thomas was martyred by a king called Mazdai (a Persian name), who objected to his queen's conversion to Christianity. On the contrary, according to the traditions of the St.Thomas Christians of Kerala, Thomas was assassinated by some enraged Brahmins who were envious of Thomas's proselytizing successes. Thomas's body was buried at Mylapore, but later it was moved to Edessa.[60]

Apart from the local traditions of the St. Thomas Christians, the earliest testimony of the presence of Christians in larger India comes from Bardaisanes' *Book of the Laws* (196 A.D.), which mentions Christians in the Kushan country.[61] Eusebius (260-340 A.D.) claims that the Alexandrian Pantainos preached Christianity in India some time about 190 A.D.; according to Eusebius, Pantainos discovered that Bartholomew (Mar Thoma?) had preceded him there and had left a Hebrew (Aramaic?) copy of the Gospel of Matthew.[62]

There are also some other early Christian testimonies that attest to the knowledge early Christians too had of India. Clement of Alexandria (d. 215), for example, writes of the Indian philosophers:

Philosophy, a thing of the highest utility, flourished in antiquity among the barbarians, shedding its light over the nations. And afterwards it came to Greece. First in its ranks were the prophets of the Egyptians; and the Chaldeans among the Assyrians; and the Druids among the Gauls; and the Samanos among the Bactrians; and the philosophers of the Celts; and the Magi of the Persians, who foretold the Savior's birth and came to the land of Judea, guided by a star. The Hindu gymnosophists are also in the number, and the other barbarians philosophers. And of these there are two classes: some of them called Samanos, and others Brahmins. And those of the Samanos who are called forest-dwellers neither inhabit cities nor have roofs over them, but are clad in the bark of trees, feed on nuts, and drink water in their hands. They know neither marriage nor begetting of children, like those now called Encratites. There are also among the Hindus those who obey the precepts of Buddha (Boutta), whom, on account of his extraordinary sanctity, they have exalted into a god.[63]

Elsewhere Clement expresses a lower opinion of the Indians' natural philosophy and cites them as an example of vain asceticism.[64] However, Clement would reverse himself later, depending on his need, and refer to the spiritual courage of the Indians manifested in their encounter with Alexander the Great.[65] The third-century *Recognitiones*, associated with Clement of Rome (d. A.D. 97), also regard the Brahmins favorably: "Similarly, among the Bactrians and in the regions of India are large multitudes of Brahmins, who, following the traditions and laws and customs of their elders, do not commit adultery or murder; neither do they worship idols nor eat meat nor get drunk nor harbor malice, but always fear God."[66]

By the third century, when the Christian Church had begun to be dominated by the Western apologists, Orientalism, or scorn for the Indians, began to creep into their thinking. Tertullian (A.D.220), who wrote some books in Greek, knew about the Indian Brahmins, but scorned their naturalness or primitivism.[67] Hippolytus included the Brahmins among the heretics outside the fold of the elect. His detailed treatment of the doctrine of the Brahmins shows that he must have had some first-hand knowledge of Indian religions. Jean Filliozat argues that Hippolytus was familiar with the *Maitri Upanishad*, and uses Hippolytus as a basis for the possibility of extensive contact between the East and the West in the first Christian centuries.[68] Prudentius (A.D.410) sees the wisdom of the gymnosophists as a symbol of vanity.[69] It is understandable that Augustine (A.D. 432) who publicly renounced his Oriental Manichean heritage should be harsh in his criticism of the Orient; he thought that no good could come out of Indian wisdom.[70] On the same issue of the Brahmins, Augustine's mentor, Ambrose, however, held a different view. In a letter to Simplicianus, Ambrose compared himself favorably to the Indian and praised the courage of the Indian Gymnosophist Calanus as he faced death.[71]

In contrast to the Western Christian Fathers, the Midwestern (Eastern, when seen from the westerly direction) Christians had profound respect towards the wisdom of India and were desirous of learning from India. Two examples are worth mentioning here. They are Bardaisanes (154-222) and Basilides (early second century), who considered themselves good Christians, though their enemies, Clement and Hippolytus, branded them as heretics and Gnostics. Basilides held the doctrine of karma and reincarnation; he was reported to have taught that even the martyrs suffered for their sins since all souls come into the world tainted with the sins of their past existence. His notion of the soul as a compound of appendages is similar to Buddhist doctrine of the *skandhas*. His view of the indescribability of God is analogous to the upanishadic teaching of the *nirguna* Brahman, who is devoid of all attributes and qualities.[72]

As Porphyry's testimony indicates, Bardaisanes was the author of a book on India from which a few citations have survived. His description of the Brahmins and the Sramanas preserved by Porphyry is quite accurate. He carefully distinguishes between Brahmin priests and Buddhist monks; the former receive wisdom by succession, by being born into a caste, while the latter receives it by choice and election. To paraphrase Porphyry:

> Of the philosophers, some dwell on mountains, others near the Ganges River. They eat fruits, cow's milk or rice, but under no circumstances touch animal food, which would denote extreme impurity and impiety. They spend their days and much of their nights in hymns and prayers to the gods. Each has his own cottage and lives for the most part alone. Often they do not speak for many days; moreover, they engage in frequent fasts....The ascetics, however, have expressly chosen their status. Anyone

wishing to join them must announce his intention to the ruler of his native place, then abandon the city and all his property. He will not return to his wife and children, or pay any further attention to them. The wife will be supported by her relatives, and the children by the king. The ascetics live outside the city and spend their days in pious conversation. They reside in houses and temples (monasteries) built for them; by the king, and of which they are stewards. Like the Brahmins they eat rice, bread, fruits, and herbs; all are unmarried and without possessions. They willingly await death, sometimes seeking it out when they are neither ill nor oppressed. Both Brahmins and ascetics are greatly revered by other Indians. The king himself visits the holy men; in times of danger he asks for their prayers.[73]

3. India's Debt to the Greeks

All that I have said about the indebtedness of the West to India may sound like a case of "Occidentalism," an expression of the Orient's superiority over the Occident as though the East had never learned or borrowed anything from the West during antiquity. Not so. Of course, the East did learn much from the West since the Renaissance but even during the Hellenistic times. Besides having learned from the Greek artists of Gandhara, India has also learned much from Greek astronomy. Early Indian scientists are quite explicit about it. "The Yavanas are indeed barbarians," says the *Gargi Samhita*, "but astronomy originated with them, and for this they must be venerated as gods."[74] Two of the five Indian astronomical treatises (*siddhantas*), the *Romaka siddhanta* and the *Paulika siddhanta* are manifestly Greek; the former is named after *Romaka* , "a famous city," which is none other than Rome, which is alluded to several times in the *Brihatsamhita* and *Pancha Siddhantika* of Varahamitra; the latter is named after Paul of Alexandria (fourth century AD.).[75] The *jamitra*, or the seventh place on the horoscope, by which the astrologer predicts happiness for the married person, is the Greek *diametron*. Similarly, many of the names of the planets and of the signs of the zodiac, like *Kriya* for the Greek *Krios*, *Tavuri* for *Tauros*, *Jituma* for *Didmos*, *Pathona* for *Parthenos*, *Ara* for *Ares*, *Heli* for *Helios*, *Asphiyit* for *Aphrodite* and *Himna* for *Hermes*, are also of Greek origin.[76] In this connection, it should be mentioned that the Greeks also knew of Indian astronomy already in the second century BC. The most astonishing piece of evidence is an inscription of the late second century BC. found during the excavations of the theater at Miletus; this calendar of the heliacal risings and settings of certain fixed stars mentions the name *ho Indon Kallaneus* in a list of earlier authorities.[77] It is fair to say that"astronomy and astrology in India are not indigenous sciences, but are local adaptations and developments of Mesopotamian, Greco-Babylonian, and Greek texts."[78]

It is possible to argue that Indian classical drama also may owe some thing to Greece since the Greek language and art were known in northwestern India. Indian drama has the word, *yavanika* ("Greek curtain"), which seems to suggest some indebtedness to Greek dramaturgy. The Indian author of the play

Toy Cart (*Mricchakatika*), a play similar to the New Attic Comedy, may have seen Greek plays performed; like the Greek critics before him, Bharata in his *Natya Sastra* lays down the rule that no more than five characters appear on the stage at the same time; the Indian *Vidushaka* and the *vita* of Indian drama can be compared to the parasite and pimp of Greek comedy; also, like the Greek plays, Indian drama eschews the portrayal of violent scenes on stage. Further, at Ramgarh, a small Greek amphitheater was unearthed.[79]

MEDIEVAL PERIOD (AD 500-1500)

Ever since the publication of Henri Pirenne's seminal study *Mahomet et Charlemagne*,[80] a consensus has emerged that Europe, Byzantium, and the Islamic caliphate created the medieval tradition in mutual interaction. More than that, as André Wink puts it, "an adequate theory of historical explanation would have to articulate an even broader framework of analysis which includes China, Central Asia, and India with the Indian Ocean at large....Clearly...the idea that the medieval world was made up of isolated civilizations is giving way to a much more intricate and interesting model in which various forms of interaction are emphasized"[81]In other words, medieval travelers, whether Jewish, Christian, or Muslim, needed one another and helped one another during their travels to India.

1. Pilgrims and Travelers (AD 500-800)

The fall of the Western Roman Empire in 476 did not altogether put an end to travel from Europe to the East. Though trade continued between Europe and the East, traders did not leave much valuable written information on the geography of Asia or India. The travelers who left important records for this period are pilgrims who trekked to Palestine and other holy places to retrace the footsteps of Jesus and his Apostles. Too often the works of these pilgrim travelers contain not only their own personal observations but also demonstrable, unacknowledged quotations from Pliny, Solinus, and some other writers of an earlier age. This is true of the writings of the pilgrim nun Etheria (fourth century), Theodosius (sixth century), and Antoninus of Placentia (sixth century).[82]. These pilgrims describe the numerous holy places and relics they visited in Palestine, Sinai, Egypt, Syria, and Mesopotamia; their travelogues are, indeed, remarkable for the extent of ground they cover.

The travel accounts of Bishop Arculf (c. 670) and Willibald (722) to the Middle East are different in the sense that they were recorded by others. Arculf's account was written down by the famous abbot of Iona, Adamnan, the biographer of St. Columba. The Englishman Willibald, later bishop of Eichstadt and nephew of St. Boniface, dictated his travel memoirs to a nun, who assures the readers that she, an unworthy child of the Saxon race, is a poor specimen of humanity (*quasi homuncula*) and a member of the corrupt weaker sex (*fragili sexus imbecillitate corruptibilis*).[83] The aforementioned pilgrims did not venture farther east because of perceived threats from Muslims; however, in the year 883, according to the Peterborough Version of the Anglo-Saxon Chronicle, King Alfred sent two emissaries, Sigehelm and Athelstan, with votive offerings to India, to the tombs of Saints Thomas and Bartholomew, to fulfill the vows he had made while in London in his war against the Vikings; these emissaries returned to England with precious stones and fragrances from India.[84]

There exist two earlier travel accounts of a missionary nature to the East including India. According to several Church historians, a philosopher of Tyre by the name Meropius set out for India about the year 330, accompanied by two young boys Aedesius and Frumentius. Somewhere on the coast of India, Meropius was assassinated, but the two boys were spared and found favor with the king of the land. Aedesius and Frumentius preached Christianity in India. After they were allowed to leave India, they returned to Tyre and Alexandria. Athanasius made Frumentius bishop of India, and later he was succeeded by an Arian bishop Theophilus, a native of the island of Diu, off the coast of Gujrat, India.[85] This Theophilus, nicknamed "Indian," seems to have gone to Byzantium during the reign of Constantine. Photius, patriarch of Constantinople from 853, quotes from the now lost *Ecclesiastical History* by the Philostorgius (354-425) that Constantius (emperor from 337-361) sent Theophilus the Indian as the head of an embassy to the Sabeans of Arabia Felix (Yemen), from where he crossed over to the island of Divus (Diu), his native land. From Diu he went to different parts of India preaching the Gospel, reforming the churches according to the Arian teaching, and correcting some practices of the Indians like the custom of sitting, instead of standing, while listening to the Gospel during the Holy Mass.[86]

The second missionary traveler of this period is the Byzantine monk Cosmas, nicknamed "Indicopleustes" or the Indian traveler. His work, *Christian Topography* written about 550, gives evidence of his travels to Ethiopia, Socotra, Sri Lanka, and India. He speaks of several Christian churches on the west coast of India and refers to the bishop of the Indian Christians as one ordained in Persia.[87]   His descriptions of the flora and fauna of India make delightful reading; some historians, however, doubt whether he ever visited India since much of the information he gives in his book could have been learnt from other travelers.[88]

2. Religion and Travel (800-1500)

Trade, pilgrimage, and proselytism were the main motivating forces behind much medieval travel to India. Naturally, the curiosity of the medieval traveler was piqued by the classical writers' descriptions of India They continued in the footsteps of the ancients who had already mapped out their travel routes. Conquest of India was hardly on their mind since they were not yet part to a military expedition but rather members of trade caravans on land routes and passengers on commercial boats.

The Jewish travelers to India were primarily merchants. Abul-Kasim-Obeidulla bin-Ahmad in his *Book of Routes and Kingdoms* composed between 844 and 848 has left a remarkable passage on the role of Jewish merchants and the state of intercommunication between Europe and Asia in the ninth century:

> The Jewish merchants speak Persian, Roman (Greek and Latin), Arabic, and the French, Spanish and Slav languages. They travel from the West to the East, and from the East to the

West, now by land and now by sea. They take
from the West eunuchs, females, slaves, boys, silk,
furs, and swords. They embark in the country of
the Franks on the Western sea and sail to Frama;
there they put their merchandise on the backs of
animals and go by land marching for five days to
Colzom.... Then they embark on the Eastern Sea
(Red Sea) and go from Colzom to Hedjaz and
Jidda; and then to Sindh, India, and China. On
their return they bring musk, aloes, camphor,
cinnamon, and other products of eastern
countries, and return to Colzom, and then to
Frama where they take ship again on the Western
Sea, some going to Constantinople to sell their
goods, and others to the country of the Franks.[89]

However, not all these travelers were
merchants or Jewish. Many were Christian
missionaries, Muslim merchants, and Buddhist
pilgrims. Some prominent Christian travelers
came from Europe. The travelers from Europe
who have left descriptions of their travels in
India were primarily merchants and/or
missionaries with the exception of John
Mandeville the tourist. Most of the Christian
missionaries, on the other hand, came from the
"Midwest "(from the Indian perspective, but
"Middle East" from the Western perspective);
they were Nestorian priests and bishops who
came to India to take care of the pastoral needs

of the immigrant and native Syrian Christians of Kerala and the rest of India; these Midwestern missionaries have not left any travel records. The Muslim missionaries and merchants also came from the Midwest. On the other hand, the Buddhist pilgrims came from the North. On account of space limitations, this study is limited to travelers from Europe, especially those from the twelfth century.

Western Christians visited India not only for the purpose of making pilgrimages to the tomb of Apostle Thomas but also in their desire to seek out the legendary kingdom of Prester John. It is known in history that a pilgrim called Saint Bernard the Penitent visited the tomb of St. Thomas between 1170 and 1177; some twenty years later Henry Morungen, a Saxon king, also visited St. Thomas's tomb. Friar Philip, the Dominican prior in Jerusalem, wrote in 1237: "I have received many letters from another person who is called Jakelinus [Catholicos] and who presides over all those Christians who are separated from the Church on account of the Nestorian heresy; his prelacy extends over greater India and the kingdom of Presbyter John."[90] The remarkable Jewish traveler from

Spain, Benjamin of Tudela, deserves special mention here.

A. Benjamin of Tudela

The Spanish Jew Rabbi Benjamin of Tudela (1159-73) has left some interesting observations on South India. The Choulam (Koulam of Marco Polo abn Battuta) that the rabbi refers to is probably the port of Kollam (Quilon). He writes about the citizens of Choulam:

> They are descendants of Khush, are addicted to astrology, and are all black. This nation is very trustworthy in matters of trade, and whenever foreign merchants enter their port, three secretaries of the king immediately repair on board their vessels, write down their names and report them to him. The king thereupon grants them security for property, which they may even leave in the open fields without any guard.[91]

The venerable rabbi was probably visiting his fellow Jews in India and the East. Among the people of Choulam, he found about one hundred black Jews, who are "good men, observers of the law and possess the Pentateuch, the Prophets and some knowledge of the Talmud and the Halakkah."[92] According to the rabbi, there were 23,000 Jews on the "island of Ibrig" (Sri Lanka)! He then goes on to describe China. It is true that the rabbi's many statements about India and China are very vague; however, it is good to note that he was the first Western writer who refers to China.

B. Marco Polo

It took Marco Polo, the Venetian traveler of the thirteenth century, three and a half years across Asia to reach the court of Kubla Khan, where he became a favorite of the Khan and spent seventeen years in the Mongol court. He left China in 1292 on his way to Persia through India to escort a princess of the Khan's family destined as bride for the Persian ruler of the time. His narrative gives valuable information on South India, where he notices fine cotton clothes, many superstitions, worship of the cow, abstinence from meat, temple dancers or *ancillae deorum* (*devadasis*), practice of sati (suttee), and self-immolation of devotees to the gods. He writes about the personal habits of the people of Kerala, which are still true today:

> It is their practice, that every one, male and female, do wash the whole body twice every day; and those who do not wash are looked down much as we look on the Patarine heretics (*Patarini*). In eating they use the right hand only, and would on no account touch their food by the left hand. All cleanly and becoming uses are ministered to by the right hand, while the left is reserved for uncleanly and disagreeable

necessities, such as cleansing the secret parts of the body and the like. So also they drink only from drinking vessels, and every man has his own, nor will any one drink from another's vessel. And when they drink they do not put the vessel to the lips, but hold it aloft and let the drink spout into the mouth. No one would on any account touch the vessel with his mouth, nor give a stranger drink with it. But if the stranger has no vessel of his own, they will pour the drink into his hands as from a cup.[93]

Marco Polo records one of the earliest legends about the death of St. Thomas. In this story of the martyrdom of the saint, there is no reference to his death at the hands of his putative Brahmin adversaries. Polo writes:

They tell that the saint was in the woods outside his hermitage saying his prayers; and round about him were many peacocks, for these are plentiful in that country than anywhere else. And one of the Idolaters of that country being of the lineage of the *Govi* [obviously not Brahmins] that I told you of, having gone with his bow and arrows to shoot peafowl, not seeing the Saint, let fly an arrow at one of the peacocks; and this arrow struck the holy man in the right side, insomuch that he died of the wound, sweetly addressing himself to the Creator. Before he came to that place where he thus died he had been in Nubia, where he converted much people to the faith of Jesus Christ.[94]

It is also remarkable in this context that Apostle Thomas's burial place in Mylapore was a famous place of pilgrimage not only for Christians but also for Muslims. "Both Christians and Saracens also do hold the saint in great reverence, and say that he was one of their own Saracens and a great prophet, giving him the title of Avarian, which is as much as to say 'Holy Man'."[95]

Marco Polo sees also flaws in the character of some Indians. He sees Indians, though idolaters, as humans with good and bad traits in their character. After he discusses the honesty, truthfulness, chastity, and abstinence of the Abraiaman (Brahmins), he talks about the practice of piracy in India:

> I assure you that these Abraiaman are the best traders in the world and the most reliable. They would not tell a lie for anything in the world and do not utter a word that is not true....They eat no meat and drink no wine. They live very virtuous lives according to their own usage. They have no sexual intercourse except with their own wives. They take nothing that belongs to

another.(277)....If any ship enters their estuaries and anchors there, they seize the ship and plunder the cargo, especially if the ship has some other destination. They say: "You were bound for somewhere else; God has directed you here that we may take what you have." They do not consider it wrong to seize the ship and her goods. This practice prevails in other provinces of India, namely, they seize even ships in distress which call on their ports. But, if the ship is bound to their ports, they give it protection.... Here is another item which is not creditable. I must tell you that this kingdom [on the west coast] is the base for many corsairs who sally out to sea and take a heavy toll of merchant shipping. And, what is more, they act with the connivance of the king. For he has struck a bargain with the corsairs that they shall give him all the horses they may capture.... And this is a shameful compact and unworthy of a king.[96]

Indian Erotic Art in Marco Polo's Eyes

Marco Polo's educated observations on the erotic temple art of Khajuraho are enlightening, I think. Therefore, a short note on this interesting topic is in order.

The studious and audacious Marco Polo had probably read or heard about the Persian scholar Al Biruni's "encyclopedic work on India composed in the eleventh century.[97] Al Biruni admits that Hindus hate Muslims the conquerors and that Muslims have a hard time understanding Hindus and their polytheistic religion. It looks like that the cosmopolitan traveler Marco Polo viewed India without the religious chip on his shoulder that the devout Muslim Al Biruni was a victim of.

Marco Polo was apparently intrigued in particular by Al Biruni's reference to Khajuraho's temples and other reports that he had heard while in India about the erotic sculptures, which were only partially mutilated by the Muslim invaders because Al Biruni's Afghan patron Muhammad of Ghasni spared the Khajuraho temples' total destruction. However, other temples in the fabled cities of India—Delhi, Kanauj, Somnath, and Mathura—fell victims to the incendiary wrath of the iconoclastic armies of the Muslim invaders. In

Mehrauli in Delhi the conquerors erected the Qutub Minar or The Tower of Victory on the site of the city's largest Hindu temple.

I have reprinted here only a few of the numerous pictures of erotic sculptures [98] found at the Khajuraha temples, which temples today number only twenty though there used to be eighty of them built by the Chandela dynasty of the Rajput kings. The sculptures on ceilings and walls display highly ornamented and full-bodied Apsaras in postures of dance and gesture. One applies kohl or mascara to her eyes; another removes a thorn from her foot, while another feeds a bird perched on her shoulder. Watching all these are gods standing formally and supporting the symbols of their identities, alongside the Asuras who appear as fantastic monsters or as elephants. They are all gazing the resplendent display of erotic scenes.

Understandably, from the financial perspective, the royal patrons and priests who had spent much money for the construction of the temples were obviously using the erotic sculptures to attract the faithful to worship at the temples so that they might make their generous donations and votive offerings of gold and silver for obtaining their desire to have children and so on, after watching the devadasis perform at the temples. The priests could justify the display of *mithuna* (sexual union) for what it is, for the pursuit of one of the noble purposes of life, which is *kama* or enjoyment, without the feeling of guilt as immortalized in *Ratirahasya* and in the Vatsyayana's *Kamasutra*.

From this very mundane or business perspective the temple priests were doing exactly what we ourselves do in the current pornographic industry of x-rated performances in gentlemen's clubs and captured in pictures and videos etc., designed primarily for making a financial profit by using/abusing sex performers. However, the Khajuraho erotica purportedly are more than a secular enterprise because they are displayed in the sacred space of temples built for worshipping deities unlike our erotic displays held far away from churches.

To sublimate sex from the secular to the sacred, one may argue that these temples were centers of tantric cult in which sexual union is celebrated as a sacrament or as a means for the union of the human with the divine. The tantrists of the Vamachara (left-hand practice) tradition emphasized enjoyment (bhoga) their principal concern by gratifying and sublimating natural inclinations in rituals. Thus sex for them is a means for transcending self. However, historically speaking, tantric cults were secret groups or organizations notorious for their erotic excesses, which one did not dare flaunt for fear of persecution. Therefore it is hard to associate Khajuraho temples with he cultic centers of tantric sex.

Admittedly, the interpretations given above contain a kernel of truth, for people go to temples for different reasons and find satisfaction and bliss according to their desires or needs. As the old saying goes, *"Id quod recipitur ad modum recipientis recipitur"* (Whatever is received, [like in the case of bottle receiving water], is received in the form and shape of the receiver). The temple priests and laborers got their monetary rewards and continued employment. As for the faithful worshippers, these sculptures promoted sex for procreation and greater enjoyment in their pursuit of *kama*. From a mystical standpoint, since sexual enjoyment can be viewed as a symbol of heavenly bliss, tantrists can argue that they celebrate sex as a sacrament.

2. Marco Polo Has a Very Different Perspective of Khajuraho Art

As early as the thirteenth century, not long after the erotic sculptures came into existence at Konarak, Polo visited the Khajuraho temples and apparently had the opportunity to talk to the contemporary artists and Brahmin scholars on location. Then as now there is agreement on the following facts or premises pertaining to Khajuraho sculptures:

1. Gods and goddesses presented in the sculptures are actual viewers or spectators at erotic performances.

2. The performers on the temple friezes are not human actors but heavenly artistes or celestial dancers like the Apsaras and Gandharvas. Their bodies were not built of the gross substance of the earth such as flesh and bones but composed of the attributes of air consisting of movement like bending, stretching, jumping, and running as the *Garuda Purana* XV.25 would have it. And the apsaras dance at the festival of gods in Indra's heaven as in *Mahabharata* III.43.28.32. During these festivals the

Gandharvas make music and join in the dance in Indra's city of Amaravati.

3. Heaven is modeled after the earth simply because we create gods in our own image and likeness; that is, heavenly apsaras do what earthly devadasis do in the temple with the difference that the apsaras are more perfect than the beautiful devadasis because the apsara body is made of heavenly substance, and they dance and perform for the enjoyment of the gods; that is, to please, pacify, and entertain the gods and goddesses.

Marco Polo tells us that the devadasis dance like the heavenly apsaras to please gods and goddesses present in the temples. Here below is the excerpt from Marco Polo's account about the devadasis and their cult in the temples:

> Let me tell you further that they have many idols in their monasteries, both male and female, and to these idols many .maidens are offered in the following manner. Their mother and father offer them to certain idols, whichever they please. Once they have been offered, then whenever the monks of these idol !monasteries require them to come to the monasteries to entertain the idol, they come as they are bidden; and sing and afford a i lively entertainment And there are

great numbers of these ! maidens, because they form large bevies. Several times a week in every month they bring food to the idols to which they are dedicated; and I will explain how they bring it and how they say that the idol has eaten. Some of these maidens of whom I have spoken prepare tasty dishes of meat and other food and bring them to their idols in the monasteries. Then they lay the table before them, setting out the meal they have brought, and leave it for some time. Meanwhile they all sing and dance and afford. the merriest sport in the world. And when they have disported themselves for as long a time as a great lord might spend in eating a meal, then they say that the spirit of the idols has eaten the substance of the food. Whereupon they take the food and eat together with great mirth and jollity. Finally they return - each to her own home. This they do until they take husbands. Such . maidens are to be found in profusion throughout this kingdom. doing all the things of which I have told you. And the reason why they are called on to amuse the idols is this. The priests of the idols very often declare: 'The god is estranged from the goddess. One will not cohabit with the other, nor will they hold speech together. Since they are thus estranged and angry with each other, unless they are reconciled and make their peace, all our affairs will miscarry and go from bad to worse, because they will not bestow their blessing and their favour.' So these maidens go to the monastery as I have said. And there, completely naked, except that they cover their private parts, they sing before the god and goddess. The god stands by himself on an altar under a canopy, the goddess by herself on another altar under another canopy. And the *people* say that he often dallies with her, and they have intercourse together; *but* when they are estranged they refrain from intercourse, and then these maidens come to placate them. When they are there, they devote *themselves* to *singing*, dancing, *leaping*, *tumbling*, and every sort of exercise *calculated* to amuse the god and goddess and to reconcile them. And *while* they are thus entertaining them, they cry: '0 Lord, wherefore art thou wroth with thy Lady? Wherefore art thou grown cold towards her, and wherefore *is* thy *spirit* estranged? Is she not comely? *Is* she not pleasant? Assuredly, yea. May it please thee, therefore, to be reconciled with her and take thy delight with her; for assuredly she is exceedingly pleasant.' And then the maiden who has spoken these words will lift her leg higher than her neck and perform a pirouette for the delectation of the god and goddess. When they have had enough of this entertainment, they go home. In the morning the idol priest will announce with great joy that he has seen the god consort with the goddess and that harmony *is* restored between them. And then everyone rejoices and gives thanks. The flesh of these maidens, so *long* as they remain maidens, *is* so hard that no one *could* grasp or pinch them in any place: for a penny they will allow a man to pinch them as hard as he can. After they are married their flesh remains hard, *but* not so hard as before. On account of this hardness, their breasts do not hang down, *but* remain upstanding and erect (171-2).

3. Marco Polo complemented

Let me complement the important findings of Marco Polo about the mystery of Khajuraho art. We are not shocked or surprised that Polo could not remember the names of any of the Hindu deities mentioned by his interlocutors simply because Polo was not a scholar of Hindu legends. But he remembered the sum and substance of what he had heard. What I doing here below is simply connecting the dots.

The central divine figures pictured below, whose marriage is celebrated or remembered every year in the Khajuraho temple complex during Maha Shivaratri, are God Shiva and Goddess Parvati. It is their love story and family love that is alluded to by Marco Polo who did not know enough legends of Shiva and Parvati to say more in detail about them. In other words, Polo simply could not remember their names and the stories about the love-separation-union-relationship of Shiva and Parvati. Briefly stated, the popular legend is as follows:

The Puranas tell the tale of Sati's marriage to

Shiva against her father Daksha's wishes. The conflict between Daksha and Shiva gets to a point where Daksha does not invite Shiva to his *yagna* (fire-sacrifice). Daksha insults Shiva, when Sati comes on her own. She immolates herself at the ceremony. This shocks Shiva, who is so grief-stricken that he loses interest in worldly affairs, retires and isolates himself in the mountains, in meditation and austerity. Sati is then reborn as Parvati, the daughter of Himavat and Mainavati,[4] and is named Parvati, or "she from the mountains", after her father Himavant who is also called king *Parvat* [mountain].

> According to different versions of her chronicles, the maiden Parvati resolves to marry Shiva. Her parents learn of her desire, discourage her, but she pursues what she wants. Indra sends the god Kama - the Hindu god of desire, erotic love, attraction and affection, to awake Shiva from meditation. Kama reaches Shiva and shoots an arrow of desire.[51] Shiva opens his third eye in his forehead and burns the cupid Kama to ashes. Parvati does not lose her hope or her resolve to win over Shiva. She begins to live in mountains like Shiva, engage in the same activities as Shiva, one of asceticism, yogin and tapas. This draws the attention of Shiva and awakens his interest. He meets her in disguised form, tries to discourage her, telling her Shiva's weaknesses and personality problems.[51] Parvati refuses to listen and insists in her resolve. Shiva finally accepts her and they get married.[51][52] Shiva dedicates the following hymn in Parvati's honor,
> I am the sea and you the wave,
> You are Prakṛti, and I Purusha.

– Translated by Stella Kramrisch[53]

After the marriage, Parvati moves to Mount Kailash, the residence of Shiva. To them are born Kartikeya (also known as Skanda and Murugan)-the leader of celestial armies, and Ganesha - the god of wisdom that prevents problems and removes obstacles.[99]

Since the physical union of Shiva and Parvati are celebrated during the holy Shivaratri at Khajuraho, we can view their and our *mithuna* (erotic embrace) as a symbol of *moksha*, which is symbolically the final release or the reunion of Purusha and Prakrti, like in the Christian apocalyptic vision of the heavenly marriage of the Lamb and the redeemed souls or as in Canticle of Canticles. Indeed, this idea is reinforced by the fact that there are several divine couples depicted in the Khajuraho temples, where there are prominent images of Vishnu standing in close embrace with his consort and Brahma holding his consort Brahmi. But the most prominent divine couple, whose ecstatic union celebrated at Khajuraho are Shiva and Parvati.

It is understandable that Marco Polo did not want to explain the erotic sculptures as expressions of the consummation of the divine wedding simply because in Polo's biblical pantheon there are no female deities. However, Polo found the idea of appeasing an angry or unhappy god as eminently acceptable even from the Christian perspective as in Genesis chapters 6 to 8. The major difference between the Indian art and biblical narrative is that for the Bible sex is the problem, while in Indian art sex is the solution. Knowing this Hindu-Christian dichotomy, Marco Polo chose the common ground found in both religions: the appeasement and pleasuring of god:

> When human beings began to increase in number on the earth and daughters were born to them, **2** the sons of God saw that the daughters of humans were beautiful, and they married any of them they chose. **3** Then the Lord said, "My Spirit will not contend with[a] humans forever, for they are mortal[b]; their days will be a hundred and twenty years."

> **4** The Nephilim were on the earth in those days—and also afterward—when the sons of God went to the daughters of humans and had children by them. They were the heroes of old, men of renown.

> **5** The Lord saw how great the wickedness of the human race had become on the earth, and that every inclination of the thoughts of the human heart was only evil all the time. **6** The Lord regretted that he had made human beings on the earth, and his heart was deeply troubled. **7** So the Lord said, "I will wipe from the face of the earth the human race I have created— and with them the animals, the birds and the creatures that move along the ground—for I regret that I have made them." **8** But Noah found favor in the eyes of the Lord Genesis 6:1-8).

> "Then Noah built an altar to the Lord and, taking some of all the clean animals and clean birds, he sacrificed burnt offerings on it. **21** The Lord smelled the pleasing aroma and said in his heart: "Never again will I curse the ground because of humans, even

though[a] every inclination of the human heart is evil from childhood. And never again will I destroy all living creatures, as I have done (8:20-21).

3. Christian Missionaries

The Mongolian conquest after 1241 of the caliphates of Baghdad and Syria created a new climate of opinion in Europe toward the East. European rulers began to perceive the Mongols no longer a threat to their existence but rather an ally against their common enemy Islam. Europeans found out that the Mongols were tolerant to all creeds: Buddhist, Hindu, Muslim, Christian, and Jewish. They also came to know about the legendary Prester John[100] and large groups of Nestorian Christians scattered throughout Asia. Rumors of Christian princesses in Mongol royal families reached European ruling houses. Dreams of converting the Great Khan to Latin Christianity and forging a Mongol-Christian alliance for the purpose of reconquering Palestine and Egypt also began to take shape in Western Christian imagination. As a result, merchants as well as missionaries went to Mongolia on diplomatic missions.[101]

Franciscan friars were the first to travel to Mongolia. John of Pian de Carpine, the Italian Friar, was sent by Pope Innocent IV in 1245 to the Great Khan, followed by William of Rubruck of Flanders from St. Louis, the king of France, to the new Khan in 1251. They were the first European writers to make the land journey to Mongolia and return. It was their travel accounts that gave merchants like the Polos the impetus and inspiration to travel to China. Indeed, missionaries took up the challenge and went all the way from Europe to India and China to convert not only heathens but also Nestorian heretics.

A. John of Monte Corvino

Already in 1291-92, while Marco Polo was on his way through the Malabar region, a Latin mission under John of Monte Corvino visited the area. Monte Corvino spent thirteen months in Malabar and baptized about one hundred persons. He later became bishop of Cambluc (Peking) and died there in 1328. His writings show very little understanding of and appreciation for the Indian culture as well as for Nestorian Christianity. His negative criticisms of India set the tone for future missionary attitudes toward the Indians. He writes:

The people of this region are idolaters, without moral law, or letters, or books....They have no consciousness of sin whatever. They have idol-houses in which they worship at almost all hours of the day, for they never join together in worship at any fixed hour,. but they go to worship their idols in any part of these temples, either by day or by night....The sin of the flesh they count not to be sin, nor are they ashamed to say so....In the region by the sea are many Saracens, and they have great influence, but there are few of them in the interior. There are a few Christians, and Jews, and they are of little influence. The people persecute the Christians and all who bear the Christian name.... They eat grossly like pigs, to wit, with the whole hand or fist, and without a spoon. In fact, when at their food they do look more like pigs than men![102]

Friar John finds the Indians in need of the civilizing touch of the Christian religion and views India as a land full of trade potential: "I have seen the greater part of India and made inquiries about the rest, and can say that it would be most profitable to preach to them the faith of Christ, if the brethren would but come.... These regions are very attractive, abounding in aromatic spices and precious stones."[103]

B. Friar Odoric

Friar Odoric (b. 1286), a Bohemian of Friuli from the town of Pordenone, was a member of the Franciscan Order. With the express intention of converting China to Christianity, he traveled from Constantinople by land through Iraq and Iran to the Persian Gulf port of Hormuz. From there he sailed to Tana near Bombay. He stayed in Tana for a little while to visit with the Christians there and to collect remains of the four Christian missionaries who were killed for their religion by some fanatic Muslims[104]. He continued his journey to Malabar in 1321 and visited Flandrina (Pantalam), Cynglin (Kayamkulam), and Polumbum (Quilon). Thence he proceeded to Sri Lanka and to the shrine of St. Thomas in Mylapore. He continued his journey through Sumatra, Java, Borneo, Champa (Campuchea), and Canton to Cambluc (Peking), where he stayed for three years. He returned to Venice in 1330 with his traveling companion Friar James the Irishman by way of Lhassa in Tibet and the Silk Route through Iran and Iraq. After these long travels, the friar retired to St. Anthony's Monastery in Padua and dictated his travel narrative to Friar William of Solagna, who wrote down the account in homely Latin. Odoric died on 14 January 1331 at Udine on his way to Avignon to visit the Pope who was in exile in France at this time.

Friar Odoric's travel account known as "The Marvels of the East" (*De Mirabilibus Indiae / De Mirabilibus Orientalium Tartarum*) became very popular in the fourteenth century. This work is considered the second best ravel book after that of Marco Polo but superior to Polo's in personal note. According to later popular accounts, he converted 20,000 Saracens to Christianity during his missionary travels. However, Odoric's book does not give the impression or evidence that he was given to much preaching; he was rather more interested in travel and sightseeing than proselytizing.

In Odoric's account Indians receive no praise at all. He writes:

> In the city of Flandrina, some of the inhabitants are Jews and some are Christians; in civil strifes, which are frequent, the Christians beat and overcome the Jews all the time.... From Malabar it is a journey of ten days to the realm of Mobar [Coromandel Coast] where there are many cities and towns. In this realm is the church where the body of St. Thomas is buried. In this church there are many idols, and beside it there are some fifteen houses of Nestorians, that is to say, Christians, but vile and pestilent heretics.[It seems that Odoric is confusing the Christian church with the temple of Mayila Devi, which is near the Christian Cathedral]...Many other things are done by that people which it would be abomination even to write or to hear of.[105]

On the contrary, Odoric writes about the Chinese with the greatest respect and admiration:

The land has great store of bread, of wine, of rice,

of flesh and fish of sorts, and of all manner of victuals whatever are used by mankind. And all the people of this country are traders and artificers, and no man ever seeks alms, however poor they be, as long as he can do anything with his own hands to help himself; but those who are fallen into indigence and infirmity are well looked after and provided with necessities. The men, as to their bodily aspect, are comely enough, but colorless, having beards of long straggling hairs like mousers (cats, I mean). However, as for the women, they are the most beautiful in the world.[106]

It is clear that Odoric left his heart in China whither he wanted to return. Perhaps the purpose of his projected visit to the court of the Pope in Avignon was to secure his permission to return to China. He ends his book with these words: "As for me, from day to day I prepare myself to return to those countries, in which I am content to die, if it pleases him from whom all good things do come."[107] Destiny prevented his return to China, and he died in Italy while on his way to see the Pope in Avignon.

C. Friar Jordanus

The French Dominican, Friar Jordanus of Séverac, followed the trail blazed by the earlier European travelers and missionaries to China. It is quite plausible that Jordanus visited India, even before the time of Friar Odoric, in 1302 with the Italian Minorites Thomas of Tolentino, James of Padua, Peter of Siena, and the Georgian Demetrius of Tblis, for two of his letters are dated 1321 (that is, a few months before the death of Dante in Italy (September 14, 1321) and 1324.[108] In his first letter he writes: "I will truly say a word as to the expected harvest, which promises to be great and encouraging for the Christian religion. Let the friars get ready and come t o three places in India: Supera, Parocco, and Columbus."[109] In spite of the fact that three missionaries were killed, he would still like to believe that the Indians have great respect for the Latin Christians and he claims that the Scriptures of the Indians prophesied the arrival of the European and that they long for it.[110] He shows, on the other hand, little regard for the Indian Christians themselves: "In this part of India there is a scattered people, one here and one there, who call themselves Christians. They are not really Christians, for they have no baptism and know hardly anything about their faith. They say that St. Thomas the Apostle is Christ."[111]

In the mind of Jordanus the Latinization and Christianization of India can and should be achieved through military might. First of all, he tells his Western allies that "the pagans of India have prophecies of their own that Latins are to conquer the whole world."[112] Secondly, he thinks that if the Pope would but establish the smallest fleet upon the Indian Ocean, great profit would be reaped from it, especially the defeat of the Sultan of Egypt: "If our lord the Pope would but establish a couple of galleys on this sea, what a gain it would be! And what damage and destruction to the Soldan of Alexandria? O, who will tell this to his Holiness the Pope?...Pray for the pilgrim of Christ, all of you, that the Indian coverts, black as they are, may all be made white in soul before the good Jesus, through his grace."[113]

Jordanus spent several years on the west coast of India long after the dispatch of his second letter. His careful observations of the flora, fauna, and the people of South India indicates that he spent considerable time in Malabar and the Coromandel Coast between 1324 and 1328. Finally he selected Columbum (Quilon) as the center of his future work. In fact, Pope John XXII appointed Jordanus bishop of Quilon in a papal brief addressed to the Nazrani Christians (*Christianis Nascarinis de Columbo*) of the place.[114]

There is no doubt that Jordanus' description of Malabar is accurate: its intolerable heat, its long rainless seasons, its naked people, its ginger and sugar cane, its beautiful parrots and peacocks, its fruits--the jack, the mango, the coconut, and so on receive the author's special attention.

In spite of his obvious prejudice against the St. Thomas Christians, he shows great respect towards the Hindus who are "true in speech and eminent in justice."[115] Indeed, Jordanus' verdict of the Indian people is substantially that of Benjamin of Tudela, Marco Polo, and John of Monte Corvino, the difference being that Jordanus talks about the use of military might for the subjugation of the people of India for the sake of financial profit and spiritual gain.

D. John de Marignoli

After the death of Friar Jordanus, an Indian Franciscan named Peter died for his Christian faith along with four other European friars in the party of Bishop Richard of Burgundy in 1340 in central Asia, as reported by John de Marignoli who traveled that route in 1341.[116]

Marignoli was the leader of the papal legation sent to the court of the Great Khan of China. Marignoli, a member of the Franciscan religious order, was consecrated bishop in 1338 and was sent with a large number (about 50) of Franciscan friars to Peking, where he spent three years (1342-45). He decided to return to Europe in 1345 and traveled via India. He arrived in Quilon in 1346, and the Christians of the city received him with great respect and treated him with royal hospitality. He preached at St. George's Latin church and claimed to have erected a marble (granite?) pillar mounted by a cross in Cape Comorin facing Adam's Peak in Sri Lanka. He did not neglect to visit the tomb of St. Thomas at Mylapore, whence he resumed his homeward journey (1349-50).

Marignoli's *Relatio* mentions the island of Sri Lanka as the location of the earthly paradise; in this conception he follows the Oriental tradition which holds the view that the golden age symbolized by the earthly paradise located in Sri

Lanka had survived the great flood that had taken place during the life of the biblical patriarch Noah. Incidentally, it is this tradition that Dante follows in his *Purgatorio* with regard to the location of the earthly paradise.

Marignoli's description of Indian trees and fruits shows that he was a careful observer. For instance, he debunks the myth of the strange creatures--the pygmies, skiopodes, cynocephali, and so on--that abound in India, according to classical geographers. He writes:

> Now to say something of the monstrous creatures, which histories or romances have limned or lied about and have represented to exist in India. ...For example, there are some folks who have but one eye in the forehead; some who have their feet turned the wrong way; some alleged to partake of the nature of both sexes, and to have the right breast like a man's, the left breast like a woman; others who have neither head nor mouth but only a hole in the breast. Then there are some who are said to subsist only by the breath of their nostrils; others a cubit in height who war with cranes. Of some it is told that they live not beyond eight years, but conceive and bear five times. Some have no joints; others lie ever on their backs holding up the sole of the only foot they have to shade them; others again have dog's heads....I never could ascertain as a fact that such races of men really do exist...The truth is that no such people do exist as nations, though there may be an individual monster here and there. Nor is there any people at all such as has been invented, who have but one foot which they use to shade themselves withal. But as all Indians commonly go naked, they are in

the habit of carrying a thing like a little tent-roof on a cane handle, which they open out at will as a protection against sun or rain....And this it is which the poets have converted into a foot.[117]

In 1353, Marignoli returned to Avignon via Baghdad, Jerusalem, and Cyprus. Though he was later appointed bishop of Bisignano in Calabria, all evidence of his literary activity indicates that he spent most of the rest of his life in the service of Charles IV, emperor of Bohemia, in Prague. He wrote the book of his travels in 1354 or 1355 while he was in Prague.[118]

E.INDIA IN MEDIEVAL IMAGINATION

As a counterpoint to the earlier section of this study on India's indebtedness to the West, I must add that during the long period of cultural contact between India and the West, the West acquired not only gold, jewelry, and spices but also absorbed quite a few cultural items such as the fiddle bow, the stirrup, the blowgun, the iconography of the water buffalo, the rhinoceros, and the elephant, and some devotional practices such as the use of the rosary.[119]   On the intellectual level, the Europe's indebtedness to India is also very significant. For example, a great many ideas found in the Greek New Testament can be easily traced to Indian religious texts and traditions.[120]   According to Albertus Magnus (thirteenth century), Indians are "very learned, as is proved by the books of philosophy and astronomy that have come to us from India"[121] About the same time, John of Spain translated al-Khwarizmi's treatise on mathematics under the title "De numero Indorum". [122] Likewise, many of the fables attributed to Aesop and several other stories found in Marie de France, Boccaccio, *Legenda Aurea, Gesta Romanorum*, and *Disciplina Clericalis* were directly or indirectly (via Arabic works) derived from India. Above all, the typical Indian, who is a fiction of Western literary imagination, the Brahmin Dindimus or the

gymnosophist of classical imagination, stood as a
symbol of natural goodness, implying the
possibility of salvation outside the institutional
Church. The idealized Indian of the medieval
imagination is a person of upright morals,
acceptable to God on account of his/her careful
observation of the natural law. This classical view
of the Indian, which originated in the Alexander
romance of Pseudo-Callisthenes (c. AD. 300) and
in its interpolations attributed to the Irish Bishop
Palladius of Helenopolis (c. AD. 400)[123], became
wide spread in Europe during the Middle Ages
through the Alexander legends.[124]

Peter Abelard (d. 1142) stands out as one of
the foremost defenders of the singular sanctity and
superior virtue of the Indian Dindimus and the
Brahmins and averred that they were worthy of
heaven even though they were not baptized
Christians.[125] The virtuous Indian Brahmin
appears as worthy of praise and salvation in the
writings of Hugh of St. Victor (twelfth century),
Geoffrey of Viterbo (twelfth century), James of
Vitry (thirteenth century), and Thomas of
Cantimpre (thirteenth century).[126] Dante in the
Paradiso also recognizes the holiness of the good
pagans of India:

> Here is a man, you say, born of a strange breed
> On the banks of Indus, where there is none to tell
> of Christ, and none to write, and none to read;
> He lives, as far as we can see, quite well
> Rightly disposed, in conduct not amiss
> Blameless in word and deed; yet infidel (19: 70-76).

The most flattering medieval portrait of the Indian Brahmin and non-Western pagans is found in the popular work *Mandeville's Travels*. Originally written in French, by 1400 the book was translated into every major European language. By 1500, the number of the *Travels* manuscripts was vast; some three hundred--in English, French, Spanish, Latin, German, Irish, Danish, Czech, Irish, and Dutch have survived; there appeared four editions of the *Travels* between 1496 and 1510. In his *Travels* Mandeville challenges the religious and moral superiority of his Euro-centric audience. He describes the Brahmins as follows:

They are good folk, honest, and of good faith and good living according to the nature of their faith. And even if they are not Christian, nevertheless by natural instinct or law they live a commendable life, are a folk of great virtue, flying away from all sins, and vices and malice, and they keep the Ten Commandments well. For they are not proud nor covetous, they are not lecherous nor gluttonous. They do nothing to another man they would not have done to themselves. They set no store by the riches of this world, or by possession of earthly goods. They do not lie, nor swear oaths for no reason, but simply say thing is, or is not....Alexander the conqueror came to their lands. "Wherefore," said they, "do you gather the riches of this world, which is transitory and cannot endure? For whether you will or not they will leave you, or you them....You should not think that anything can endure for ever, except God who made all the world. And yet, not having any regard to this, you are so presumptuous and proud, that, just as if you were God, you would make all the world subject to yourself."...When Alexander heard these words, ...he ...was greatly ashamed and went away from them and did them no hurt. And even if these people do not have the articles of our faith, nevertheless I believe that because of their good faith that they have by nature, and their good intent, God loves them well and is well pleased by their manner of life.[127]

It is interesting to note that Mandeville, unlike all other earlier European travelers, does not condemn sati (suttee) but rather says that the pagans take heaven seriously (124). He even draws a moral from the violent devotion of devotees who kill themselves before the Juggernaut (Jagannath):

> Some out of great devotion to that idol fall down in front of the chariot and let it roll over them. And so some of them are slain, some have their arms and legs broken; and they believe that the more pain they suffer here for the love of that idol, the more joy they will have in the other world and the nearer God they will be. And truly they suffer so much pain and mortification of their bodies for love of that idol that hardly would any Christian man suffer the half--nay, not a tenth--for love of Our Lord Jesus Christ. (125-126).

According to Mandeville, not only the Brahmins, but also the Saracens (61), Buddhist Tibetans (186), the Jacobite Christians (79) practice a real devotion despite the fact that they are not Latin Christians. Such a view of the East is in sharp contradiction to the view of earlier missionary travelers like Jordan's who loathed the Nestorians and Rubruck who saw all Eastern religions as diabolic aberrations. In short, Mandeville confirms the conventional Western view of the Indian Brahmin as an example of natural goodness and heroic virtue and as the symbolic representative of the quintessential Indian.

INDIA IN THE AGE OF "DISCOVERY": DECLINE AND THE DEMISE OF A MYTH

While the ancient and medieval travel writers bestowed on India the myth of the virtuous Brahmin, the colonial travelers "dis-covered" the old myth and discarded it by replacing it with a new of myth of the "vicious" Indian.   This transformation of the Indian went through a stage during which opposite myths coexisted in European imagination until one was replaced by the other, which eventually spelled the decline and death of the high reputation of the mythical "Indian" of the classical and medieval writers.

Several English works from the fifteenth century like Thomas More's *Utopia*, the alliterative *Alexander and Dindimus*, the *Prose Life* of Alexander, and Trevisa's translation of Higden's *Polychronicon* also uphold the reputation of people like the Indians who live without the light of Christian Revelation.[128]   But not all writers of the period shared John Mandeville's or Thomas More's Utopian enthusiasm for the possibility of virtuous life for the Indians and non-Christians.   For example, John Rastell, Thomas More's brother-in-law, in his interlude *The Nature of the Four Elements* make his characters view the Indians not as exemplary models of virtue for the Christians to emulate but rather as people to be conquered:

O what a thynge had ben than, yf that they that be
englyshe men
Myght haue ben the furst of all
That there shulde haue take possessyon...
And also what an honorable thynge
Bothe to the realme and the kinge
To haue had his domynyon extendynge
There into so farre a grounde.[129]

In Rastell's view such a conquest is for the
good of the Indians who are savages without the
knowledge of God, Devil, Heaven, Hell, writing,
and scriptures:

And what a great meritoryouse dede
It were to haue the people instructed
To liue more vertuously,
And to lerne to knowe of men the maner
And also to knowe god theyr maker,
which as yet lyue all bestly;
For they nother knowe god nor the deuell
Nor neuer harde tell of heuen nor hell,
wrytynge nor other scrypture. [130]

Rastell heralds the view that Indians lack
moral virtue and material civilization both of
which should be bestowed on them by the
Europeans. Not surprisingly, Rastell interprets the
nakedness of the Indians or their primitivism not
as a sign of natural goodness, but as a sign of their
need for better instruction and improved
technology.

We find a similar change in the views and
consequent behavior of Columbus, as noted in the
introduction, with regard to the "Indians." In his

first encounter Columbus found the Indians to be wonderful human beings: morally upright, charitable, generous, and worshipful:

> They are exceptionally plain and of good faith and most generous with all they own. They show a profound love towards all; they give much in exchange for little; indeed, they are content with the smallest portion, or even with nothing at all....They worship no idol, but instead believe steadfastly that all strength, all power, and all good are in heaven.....They are not lazy or uncivilized, but they show heightened and perceptive wit....I found nothing monstrous among them, as many people had expected; instead, I found them almost respectful and peaceful people.[131]

However, Columbus's later repressive colonial policy resulted in the death of some one hundred thousand natives between 1494 and 1496 and the extinction of the Tainos. According to the testimony of Bartolomé de Las Casas, between 1492 and about 1540, more than twelve million Indians succumbed under the Spanish lash.[132]

The changing attitude toward the natives can be detected in the words and deeds of another explorer Vespucci, who calls the natives savage, barbarous, inhuman, bestial and wild (*immansueti, barbarus, inhumanus, bestialis, feralis,* and *brutalis*).[133] Vespucci's plan was to capture as many natives as possible and sell them as slaves, and his first letter states that at Cadiz he had two hundred and twenty-two captives sold as slaves.[134]

In the writings also of the sixteenth-century

travelers to India we see a similar change of attitude towards the Indians, especially toward the legendary Brahmins. Duarte Barbosa (1518), a cousin of Magellan, who spent several years in India, writes about the esteem the Brahmins have in the Indian society:

> They have great honor among the Indians... Some of these Bramenes serve the kings in every manner except in arms. No man may prepare any food for the king except a Bramene or his own kin; they also serve as couriers to other countries with letters, money or merchandise, passing wherever they wish to go in safety, and none does them any ill, even when the kings are at war. These Bramenes are learned in their idolatry, and possess many books thereof. The kings hold them in high esteem."[135]

> However, actual dealings with Indians convinced Barbosa and other European travelers that not all Indians, even the Brahmins, are as holy as they were thought to be. Brahmins, he says, "administer and direct idolatry," and he labels the Indians, probably after his experiences with the shrewd Banya merchants [Baneanes] of Gujarat, as "great usurers and falsifiers of weights and many other goods and coins."[136]

The famous Portuguese missionary St. Francis Xavier expresses a similar contempt for the Brahmins in his letter to the Society of Jesus (1543):

> We have in these parts a class of men among the pagans who are called Brahmins. They...are as perverse and wicked a set as can anywhere be found....They are liars and cheats to the very backbone. Their whole study is how to deceive most cunningly the simplicity and ignorance of the people.[137]

The right policy of the Colonial powers, according to Xavier, is "the spreading of our holy Faith."[138]. In the propagation of the Catholic Faith, Xavier resorted to the practice of destroying the Hindu temples: "When all are baptized I order the temples of their false gods to be destroyed and the idols to be broken in pieces. I can give you an idea of the joy I feel in seeing this done, witnessing the destruction of idols by the very people who but lately adored them."[139]

Both missionaries and colonial administrations helped accelerate the process of dethroning the icon of the noble Indian. Such a transformation of the noble and virtuous natives into ignorant and wild savages to be enlightened and encultured by civilization fell to the lot of the colonial administration who used every means to subjugate them. In this effort the Spaniards and the Portuguese resorted to the well-established principle of the Crusades that war conducted in the interests of Holy Church was automatically just.[140] In fact, within two years after the fall of Constantinople to the Ottoman Turks (1453), the Portuguese received a mandate from Pope Nicholas V who gave the king of Portugal the right to seize the lands and property of "all Saracens and pagans whatsoever, and all other enemies of Christ wheresoever place."[141] Naturally, the Portuguese used the Pope's orders to justify their raids on the Moslems in the Mediterranean and on the African coast, and on the Hindus and Muslims in India. Spain joined the Portuguese mission of plunder under the pretext of piety when Rodrigo Borgia (Pope Alexander VI) granted to the rulers of Spain all the world not possessed by the Christian states so that all the heathens might "embrace the Catholic faith and be trained in good morals."[142]   On the other hand, England cared not to wait for papal orders and decided to shed the moral mask when the Catholic monarch Henry VII commissioned John Cabot to "conquer, occupy, and possess" the lands of "heathens and infidels."[143] Thus, the decline and fall of the noble Indians was complete and the stage was set for their conquest and subjugation by the end of the sixteenth century in Western imagination, and, as a result, Europeans self-consciously announced in the seventeenth-century Hobbesian state that 'We look down upon them with scorn and Disdain and think them little better than Beasts in Human Shape.'"[144]

Perhaps the best dramatized colonial portrayal of the newly depraved Indian in the eyes of the colonial conquerors is that of Caliban in Shakespeare's *The Tempest*. In the play Caliban appears as "a salvage and deformed slave"; in Prospero's eyes he is a "misshapen knave;/[whose] mother was a witch" (5.1.268-269); he is "filth" (1.2.348); he is "a devil, a born devil" (4.1.186); the implied superiority of the European is signaled in Prospero's denial of the "brutish" Caliban's claim to the island ("This island's mine, by Sycorax my mother,/which thou tak'st from me" (1.2.333-334)): "Abhorred slave,...When thou didst not, savage, /Know thine own meaning, but wouldst gabble like / A thing most brutish, I endowed thy purposes / With words that made them known" (1.2.352-360). Needless to argue that there are enough allusions in the play to suggest that Shakespeare did not necessarily hold Prospero's or the other characters' views of Caliban, as I shall show below.

SHAKESPEARE'S DISSENTING VOICE AGAINST COLONIALIST MISPERCEPTIONS IN *THE TEMPEST*

Shakespeare's colonial discourse is very much akin to the spirit of contemporary post-colonial discourse. It is on account of Shakespeare's anti-colonial spirit that I apply the term "post-colonial" to Shakespearean discourse in the following pages.

THE "DIVINE"[i] CALIBAN IN SHAKESPEARE'S POST-COLONIAL DISCOURSE: A RE(DE)CONSTRUCTION

Miranda: What foul play had we that we came from thence?

Or blessed was't we did?

Prospero: Both, both, my girl:

By foul play as thou say'st, were we heav'd thence;

But blessedly holp hither. *The Tempest* I.2.60-64.

"Characters are self-explanatory. Here [in Caliban's case] I was mistaken." --Herbert Beerbohm Tree (1904)

Introduction

During the last four hundred years of Caliban criticism, Alden and Virginia Vaughn note in their book *Shakespeare's Caliban: A Cultural History* (1991) note, "each age has appropriated and reshaped him [Caliban] to suit its needs and assumptions, for Caliban's image has been incredibly flexible, ranging from an aquatic beast to a noble savage, with innumerable intermediate manifestations (ix). Indeed, so far the image of Caliban has been that of a beast-like but noble savage of considerable anthropological and colonial interest. In this study, after tracing the well-attested anthropological, colonial dimension of Caliban, I shall show that Shakespeare ascribes to Caliban a "blessed" or divine dimension primarily from Shakespeare's classical sources hitherto unrecognized and unacknowledged by the scholarly community and that Shakespeare embeds his mythological subtexts within his own unique anti-colonial discourse, which is post-colonial in spirit.[1]

Over the years Shakespearean scholars have done magnificent work in the intertextual criticism of *The Tempest*. Though the play's sources are notoriously uncertain, Geoffrey Bullough, Frank Kermode, Stephen Orgel, and a host of other editors and scholars have identified several anthropological and classical sources; for example, William Strachey's *True Repertory* (1625) of Thomas

Gate's Bermuda shipwreck, redemption, and arrival in Viriginia; Michel de Montaigne's essay on noble savages translated by John Florio (1603); and Sylvester Jourdain's *A Discovery of the Bermudas* (1610).[2] The passage in Ovid's *Metamorphoses* VII on Medea in Golding's translation of 1567 provides some of the witch-like features of Sycorax, Caliban's mother, and for Prospero's valedictory invocation of the spirits. Shakespeare also drew from Virgil's story of Dido and Aeneas (*Aeneid* II, III, V) for the notorious exchange about Dido in 2.1.75-86, for Ariel and his spirits appearing as harpies at Alonso's banquet (3.3), for the storm (1.1) and for the chess scene between Ferdinand and Miranda (5.1.172-75).[3]

Colonial Construct

By and large traditional scholarship has tended to view *The Tempest*-text as autotelic, as fixed in history, as produced within historical limitations, or as "an entity which always remains the same from one moment to another" (Hirsch 46). Accordingly, most critics see the play as taking place in the early phases of the Western colonization of the New World and bearing traces of the West's colonial policy. They have drawn attention to Shakespeare's own association with the prominent members of the Virginia Company and to the play's productions at the expansionist Jacobean court in 1611 and 1612-15 (Brown 48). Though Kermode discounts the centrality of colonialism in the play, New Historicist revisionists see the play as grounded in the historical events of

English colonialism and find the New World material as central to the play. Meredith Ann Skura writes:

The revisionists look not at the New World material in the play but to the play's effect on power relations in the New World.... If Caliban is at the center of the play, it is not because of his role in the play's self-contained structure ... but because Europeans were at that time exploiting the real Calibans of the world, and *The Tempest* was part of the process (44-45).

Though there is no total agreement on what Caliban is and where he comes from, most people continue to see Caliban in the colonial context as though the text were semantically fixed along with the image and meaning of Caliban. In post-colonial theatrical versions, for instance, Caliban has been interpreted as a Virginian Indian, as a black slave or as "missing link" (half-monster and half-coconut in costume) (Griffiths 159-80). Apart from connecting Caliban to the decadent Jacobean politician Robert Cecil and to mobs in Roman/Elizabethan England, Arden, Oxford, and Pelican editors of the play see Caliban more or less as monster, African slave, and dispossessed Indian.[4] It is true that all these views can find support--some more than others--in the play, the reaon being that "the play is notoriously slippery" (Skura 47). One critic, Corona Sharp, reads Caliban, in a wholly sympathetic light, as someone equal to Prospero in morality, imagination, and intellect.[5] She sees so many virtues in Caliban and denies that Caliban is a noble savage (283, n.35).

Corona is probably correct, as I shall show below.

By and large, the critical portrait of Caliban as a genuine anthropos has had a twofold dimension: (1) the salvage wild man and (2) the Native American. The wild man, the wodewose, or the green man in Britain/England--Kentigern and Merlin are two of them--was a familiar figure in folklore, painting, heraldry, pageant, and drama. Richard Bernheimer defines the wild man as "a hairy man curiously compounded of human and animal traits, without however sinking to the level of an ape" (Bernheimer 1 and Goldsmith 481-491). He is more human than beast; he has the body of a man, having the habits of animals living in animal environment. He is a satyr-type, like Bremo who abducts a virgin in *Mucedorus*, a play revived by Shakespeare's company in 1610 (Kermode xxxix). He is the *Wildemann* in Germany, *l'homme sauvage* in France, *selvaggi* in Italy (Vaughn 62-65) In fact, the term *salvage* is used of Caliban in the Folio "Names of the Actors"; Ben Jonson refers to Caliban as "servant-monster" in *Bartholomew Fair* (1614). However, by the end of the nineteenth century, scholars, after reading more colonial travel literature, began to perceive Caliban as a portrait of the Native American. This Americanization of Caliban was based on the fairly firm ground that Shakespeare was familiar with and incorporated information from Florio's translation of Montaigne's essay "Of Cannibals" and travel reports and pamphlets. Montaigne's savage, naturally virtuous Indians, uncorrupted by civilization, do not fare well in the eyes of

Prospero, who sees Caliban as "a devil, a born devil (4.1.189)." Sidney Lee declared in 1898:

Caliban is no precise presentation of any identifiable native American. He is an imaginary composite portrait, an attempt to reduce the aboriginal types.... Traits of the normal tractable type of Indian to which the Virginian and Caribbean belonged freely mingled in the crucible of his [Shakespeare's] mind with those of the irredeemable savages of Patagonia ... Shakespeare's American ... is a human being endowed with live senses and appetites ... with some control of the resources of inanimate nature and of the animal world (295-6).

Walter A. Raleigh, concurring, asserts that Caliban "is a composite wrought from fragments of travellers' tales and shows a wonderfully accurate and sympathetic understanding of uncivilized man" (13).

Leslie Fiedler, one of the early post-colonialist critics, sees the themes of colonialism and race in *The Tempest*, and identifies Caliban with the dispossessed Native American and finds in him vestiges of the African slave and the European wild man:

> To say that Caliban was for Shakespeare an Indian means that he was a problem.... *The Tempest* must be understood as an attempt to answer that troubling question on the basis of ancient pre-conceptions and new information about the inhabitants of the Americas .... [T]he point is to identify him with a kind of subhuman freak imagined in Europe even before the discovery of red men in America; *homme sauvage* or

"savage man," "who, in the nightmares of Mediterranean humanists, had been endowed with sexual powers vastly in excess of their own. Such monstrous virility Shakespeare attributes to Caliban, associating him not with cannibalism after all, but unbridled lust (233-4).

Indeed, Fiedler echoes the colonialist propaganda of the "unbridled lust"--often supposedly due to hot climate--of the natives, who have to be subjugated in order to protect the virtue of the colonial women. Though Fiedler discounts the cannibalism of the natives, scholars and readers still associate Caliban semantically with cannibalism, a far more powerful colonial propaganda tool than the unscientific allegation of unbridled sexuality used for the oppressive control of the indigenous peoples.

Homi Bhabha agrees with Fiedler's twofold dimension of the discourse of colonial power-- racial and sexual.[6] Bhabha writes:

The black is both savage (cannibal) and yet the most obedient and dignified of servants (the bearer of food); he is the embodiment of rampant sexuality and yet innocent as a child; he is mystical, primitive, simple-minded and yet the most worldly and accomplished liar, and manipulator of social forces (170).

He defines Fiedler's notion of colonial discourse as an apparatus of power and argues that the objective of colonial discourse is to construe the colonized as a population of degenerate types on the basis of racial origin, in order to justify conquest (Bhabha 154).[7] In fact, cannibalism serves as the benchmark for the native's state of degradation in the colonial discourse of *The Tempest*.

Caliban's name is etched in popular and literary imagination with the image of the Caribbean anthropophagi. Supporters of this view would say that in Shakespearean times "carib" and "cannibal" were familiar terms. Already in Columbus's days, some natives were referred to as "caribes," and "friendly" natives reportedly told Columbus that their enemies were "cannibales," providing the colonial rulers the rationale to divide and conquer their enemies.[8]

Caliban is usually taken as an anagram of "cannibal," which word seems to imply the act of eating humans as in "Cannibals that each [other] eat/The Anthropophagi (*Othello* 1.3.143-4) and in "And he had been cannibally given/He might have boiled and eaten him too" (*Coriolanus* 4.5.200-01). In 1778, Richard Farmer proposed: "The metathesis in *Caliban* from *canibal* is evident."[9] In 1821, Edmond Malone concurred: "*Caliban*, as was long since observed by Dr. Farmer, is merely the metathesis of *canibal*" (15). Though Furness dissented about the etymology of *Caliban*, he admitted in 1892: "Dr. Farmer's derivation of this name as a metathesis of *cannibal* has generally been accepted" (5). According to the *OED*,

> Professor J. H. Trumbull, of Hartford, has pointed out that *l*, *n*, and *r* interchange dialectally in American languages, whence the variant forms of *Caniba*, *Caribe*, *Calibi*, and that Colmbus's first representation of the

name as he heard it from the Cubans was *Canibales* ...
Columbus says, 'they call *Caniba*, but in Hyati *Carib*'.
Apparently, however, it was only foreigners who made
a place-name out of that of the people: according to
Oviedo (*Hist. Gen.*II.viii) *caribe* signifies 'brave and
daring', with which Prof. Trumbull compares the
Tupi *caryba* 'superior man, hero, *vir*'. *Caliban* is
apparently another variant =*carib* -*an* (s.v.
"Cannibal").[10]

The *OED* also refers to a possible figurative
usage of cannibal "as a strong term of abuse for
"bloodthirsty savage" ('cannibal' 1b), merely to a
savage or primitive person, not one necessarily
involved in anthropophagy; Shakespeare himself
provides support to this view: 'cannibals/How
sweet a plant have you untimely cropped'" (*3
Henry VI*, 5.5.61-62)."[11]   On the basis of the late
emergence of *cannibal* in print, the confusion of the
Taino with the Caribs, and the word's figurative
meaning, the Vaughans ask: "Would Shakespeare
have chosen an anagram of 'cannibal' for a savage
who did not practice what his name preached."
(30). They conclude: "A close alternative
explanation is that 'Caliban,' as an extended
anagram of 'carib,' suggests that Shakespeare
meant the monster to be a New World native but
not necessarily a man-eater" (27). Meredith
Skura's observation on the semantic implications
of *Caliban-cannibal* is very perceptive:

> Take the deceptively simple example of Caliban's
> name. Revisionists rightly emphasize the implications
> of the cannibal stereotype as automatic mark of Other
> in Western ethnocentric coloinialist discourse, and,

since Shakespeare's name for "Caliban" is widely accepted as an anagram of "cannibal," many read the play as if he *were* a cannibal, with all that the name implies. But an anagram is not a cannibal, and Shakespeare's use of the stereotype is hardly automatic. Caliban is no cannibal--he barely touches meat, confining himself, more delicately roots, berries, and an occasional fish; indeed, his symbiotic harmony with the island's natural food resources is one of his most attractive traits. His name seems more like a mockery of stereotypes than a mark of monstrosity (51-52).

Caliban can be viewed also an anagram of *cainiban* /"Cain's son." In the Jewish and Christian biblical tradition, Cain is considered the son of the devil: "Not as Cain who is of the Wicked One" (1 John 3:12); one familiar Jewish tradition depicts Cain as the son of the devil and Eve. Tertullian speaks allegorically, "Having been conceived of the seed of the Devil, she [Eve] immediately through the fecundity of evil gave birth to Anger, her son" (*De Patientia*, 5). In later traditions, Cain is portrayed as a cannibal and drinker of blood; for example, in the pseudepigrapha of "The Book of Adam and Eve," Cain drinks Abel's blood after the murder. In the Book of Enoch, blood-drinking and cannibalism are associated with the progeny of Cain.[12]

From another perspective, Caliban, as a combination of the Sanskrit/Gypsy word *cala/cali* (dark) could also mean "the dark one"--Prospero calls him "a thing of darkness"--or the son of the Mother Goddess Kali.[13]   Indeed, deconstructive critical strategy will show that Caliban's name is an ingenious pun and a mockery of stereotypes.

Deconstruction

Contemporary critics place greater stress than the New Critics on the need to anchor the text to its contexts discovered through historicism and intertextuality. Tony Bennet, for example, calls for texts to be articulated with new texts, socially and politically mobilized in different ways within different class practices." Barker and Hulme think that this critical strategy depends "on a form of intertextuality which identifies in all texts a potential depends on a form of intertextuality which identifies in all texts a potential for new linkages to be made and thus for new political meanings to be constructed."[15] It is possible to construct meanings that are already in the text with the help of subtexts hitherto overlooked by critics without necessarily ascribing to the text's meanings derived from one's own ideological prejudices. I propose to do just that by providing an "alternate"--not an "alternative"-- Shakespearean post-colonial reading of Caliban with the help of the mythological subtexts embedded in the play by Shakespeare himself, without displacing the dominant colonial discourse used by the characters of the play.

As mentioned earlier, intertextual critics have shown affinities only between the *The Tempest* and *The Aeneid* as well as *The Metamorphoses*. However, if we place the play in the wider matrix of classical mythology, the multi-dimensionality of the play's characters, especially of Caliban, will emerge in a clearer light. I shall illustrate this alternate view by showing the mythological dimensions of Caliban and of the other characters of the play.

Shakespeare bestows on Caliban the divine dimensions of the Greco-Roman Hephaestus/Vulcan/Mulciber, the god of fire and the smithy; Caliban is a Vulcan-figure in game plan and name game.[16] Shakespeare also weaves an elaborate mythological play-text around Caliban. Shakespeare's plan seems to involve a modified enactment of several Olympian dramas-- like the masque in the play with Iris, Juno, and Ceres--involving Jupiter, Juno, Vulcan, Mars, and Pandora. I shall try to unravel the various threads of the mythological subtexts by first describing the classical gods and their deeds insofar as they are related to the play and relate them to the characters who play the roles of these gods.

Classical Deities vs. Characters in the Play

Vulcan vs. Caliban

Vulcan is the god of fire, and his favorite home is the island of Lemnos. His parents are Jupiter and Juno. He is lame and awkward in his movements so that he becomes occasionally ludicrous in the eyes of the immortals (*Iliad* 1: 590-600). Twice he was thrown down from heaven, once by Juno because he was lame and the second time by Jupiter when he ran afoul of his father's wrath while defending his mother Juno. He fell into the sea but was rescued by the Naiads Thetis and Euronyme, who kept him in a cavern beneath the sea for seven years; he made fine ornaments at his smithy. Angry with his mother for casting him out of heaven, Vulcan trapped her on a golden throne with invisible, unbreakable fetters. When Mars' threats failed to move Vulcan, Bacchus got him drunk and persuaded him to release his mother from her captivity. Later Vulcan offered rich marriage gifts to Jupiter for the hand of Venus (*Odyssey* 8: 266 ff), who spurned the deformed Vulcan's advances, preferring the handsome Mars instead. Nonetheless, Vulcan continued to love the unloving Venus, and the divine couple became the parents of Palaemonius, the lame argonaut. According to another well-known myth, once Vulcan caught Mars and Venus together in his marriage bed with a fine, invisible mesh to the voyeuristic delights of the Olympians and to the wrath of the Father God. Another time, when Minerva, the goddess of wisdom and of war, came to Vulcan's forge for weapons, he tried to rape her; his seed fell on her leg, which she brushed off; the seed fell on Mother Earth, giving birth to Erichthonius. Additionally, according to *The Iliad* (18: 382), Grace (Charis) is Vulcan's wife.

Caliban is a Vulcan-figure. There are many allusions in the play as to the Caliban-Vulcan association. For example, Shakespeare echoes Vulcan's fall in:

Caliban: "Hast thou not dropped from heaven ?
Stephano: "Out o' the moon, I do assure thee: I was the man

I' the moon when time was.
Caliban: "I have seen thee in her, and I do adore thee"
(2.2.137-40).

Though Caliban refers to Stephano as the man who dropped out of the moon, implied in this passage is possibly an allusion to Vulcan's own fall from heaven.

In spite of the general perception that Vulcan is generally seen as the son of Jupiter and Juno, later traditions state that Vulcan is a bastard because Juno conceived him independent of Jupiter, with the help of the wind and her imagination because she was jealous of the unaided birth of Minerva from the forehead of Jupiter. Shakespeare is probably referring to this context when he says that Caliban is "a bastard one" (5.1.273).

Like Vulcan, Caliban is physically handicapped by lameness. Caliban's grotesqueness is mentioned several times in the play as in "this misshapen knave" (5.1.268), "lame beggar" (2.2.30), and "He is disproportion'd in his manners/As in his shape" (5.1.290-1). Vulcan's punishment by Jupiter for taking the side of Juno seems to be suggested in Caliban's fear of punishment by Prospero: "He will chastise me" (5.1.263) and "I shall be pinch'd to death" (5.1.277). Of course, Prospero punished Caliban by casting him out of his cell.

When Vulcan was thrown down from heaven, he ended up falling into the sea, from where Thetis and Euronyme rescued him and lodged him in a rock cave. In the play, Caliban's house is the "hard rock" (1.2.345, 362). The fish-references to Caliban, made several times in the play (3.2.25; 2.1.25-26; 3.2.28; 5.1.266), appropriately point to Vulcan's fall into the sea and his life with the Naiads under the water. Interestingly, the Naiads appear in 4.1.128. The fish metaphor could also be an allusion to Mars' transformation into a fish.

Caliban's name "moon-calf" (3.2.20) is significant because Vulcan is the son of the Moon Goddess Juno, who also appears in mythology as a cow; for instance, when Juno and the other gods fled to Egypt to avoid capture by the Titans, the goddess assumed the shape of a cow.

Caliban's work is similar to Vulcan's. Vulcan worked with fire and made lightning and bolts of thunder for Jupiter; Prospero assigns Caliban to the job of making fire (1.2.313-4). Vulcan wrought many wonderful works of art for gods and humans, like the palace of Helios, the golden cup of Helios, the armor of Achilles, the necklace of Harmonia, and the woman Pandora. Prospero says to Caliban: "Go, sirrah, to my cell... / Trim it handsomely" (5.1.291-3).

As Vulcan was accused of the attempted rape of Minerva, Caliban was accused of having attempted to rape Miranda. Prospero fulminates at Caliban:

> Thou, most lying slave,
> Whom stripes may move, not kindness! I've used thee,
> In mine own cell, till thou didst seek to violate
> The honor of my child (1.2.346-9).

Caliban: Oho, oho! would't had been done!
Thou didst prevent me; I had peopled else
This isle with Calibans (1.2.351-3).

In the Greek myth, Vulcan's seed fell on Gaia and produced Erichthonius; one of Vulcan's sons was the lame Argonaut Palaemonius, appropriately prefiguring Claliban's boast of wanting to produce other Calibans, probably lame like himself.

As Bacchus once managed to get Vulcan drunk in order to get him to release his mother Juno from her fetters, in the play Stephano and Trinculo succeeded in getting Caliban drunk ("My man-monster hath drown'd his tongue in sack" (3.2.11) so that he might help them kill Prospero. The Caliban-Stephano-Trinculo plot to murder Prospero during his siesta is also like Vulcan's plan to capture Mars with Venus in bed, which succeeds, whereas the former plot fails.

Vulcan had the non-pareil Venus for a wife, who was judged by Paris to be more beautiful than Juno and Minerva. Probably Caliban wanted to make Miranda his wife, who is more beautiful than Sycorax, the Juno-figure in the play. Caliban proclaims:

> The beauty of his daughter; he himself
> Calls her a non-pareil: I never saw a woman,
> Only Sycorax, my dam and she;
> But she far surpasseth Sycorax
> As great'st does least (3.2.97-101)

Indeed, Shakespeare succeeds in bringing

Venus also into the play in the masque scene (4.1.87-101), where he refers to her as "Mars's hot minion [lustful mistress] (4.1.98), the implication being that Miranda is a Venus figure not only in beauty but also in lustful behavior.[17]

According to one tradition, Vulcan is married to Grace; Shakespeare alludes to this marriage union of Vulcan and Grace in Caliban's vow "to seek grace" (5.1.295). The Graces (Thalia--bloom of life, Aglaia--brilliance, and Euphrosyne--joy) live on Mount Olympus with the Muses, and Vulcan is married to one of them; Shakespeare is probably exploiting the association of the Graces with Caliban in order to assign some of the finest lines of poetry in the play to Caliban.[18]

The many affinities between Vulcan and Caliban naturally have encouraged me to formulate the theory that Caliban might also be an anagram of Vulcan/Mulciber. All the letters of *Caliban* are found in the *Vulcan-Mulciber* compound; the *v* of Vulcan is interchangeable with *b* in New World Spanish as in *Havana/Habana; b* and *i* of *Caliban* are supplied by *Mulciber*. The shift from Vulcan/Mulciber to Caliban was probably deliberate "as with the analogous metathetic name-change from *Fastolphe* to *Falstaff* in the Henry plays" (Fleissner 297). The Vulcan-Caliban receives sufficient support in the overwhelming similarities found between the mythical god-figure and New World native, who appears to live both on a Caribbean island and on a Mediterranean island like Vulcan's Lemnos, not far from Tunis and Carthage and the Aegean, the play area of the classical gods and goddesses.

Mars/Ares vs. Ariel

The Vulcan-Caliban nexus garners also additional support from the supporting cast of Ariel, Miranda, Prospero, Sycorax, and Setebos. Vulcan's half-brother Mars--partly the inspiration behind Ariel-- rushed like whirlwind through contending forces, paying little heed to right and wrong. Once, when Diomede, aided by Minerva, inflicted a deep wound on Mars during the Siege of Troy, he fled the battlefield "roaring like ten-thousand men"; Jupiter grudgingly let Paean heal the wound but only after reminding Mars that his brawling nature was an inheritance from Mother Juno (*Iliad* V: 859-91). Once the giants Otos and Ephialtes chained Mars/Ares in bonds too strong for him to break, and he stayed thirteen months in a brazen cauldron in fuming impotence until Hermes/Mercury released him on Zeus' orders (*Iliad* V:385-91). According to another story, when the Giant Typhon attacked the gods, the defeated Olympians fled to Egypt, with Mars changing himself into a fish.

Shakespeare has cleverly hidden the identity of Ariel by giving him a biblical name (Isaiah 29:1-2). As for Ariel, Shakespeare seems to have had in mind also two other theories on the fairies--as demons or fallen angels and as an English fairy connected to "classical nymphs, fauns, hamadryads, and so forth" (Kermode 144). As Kermode reminds us, "many elements are mixed in Ariel and his strange richness derives from the mixture" (143). How correct and perceptive! I suggest that the classical god Ares (the Greek counterpart of the Roman Mars) is part of the Ariel mix because the Ariel-Ares valency throws much light on the following passages.

1. Ariel was imprisoned for twelve years by Sycorax in a cloven pine, "where thou didst vent thy groans/As fast as mill-wheels strike..." (1.2.280-1). Prospero, who alone has the power to free him from the pine-prison, finally sets him free. This story of Ariel is also closely related to the Homeric episode about Ares' agonizing groans after he was wounded by Diomede in the Trojan War and about his imprisonment by the Giants Otos and Ephialtes in a brazen cauldron from which Mercury released him after thirteen months.

2. The most obvious Ares-allusion, differences notwithstanding, is in the plot of Caliban-Stephano-Trinculo, who try to kill Prospero in his sleep (3.2.59-113). As mentioned before, Vulcan caught Mars in bed with Venus (Mars' hot minion" 4.1.98).

3. The myth of Venus's rejection of lame Vulcan for handsome Mars is similar to Miranda's--a Venus figure ("Most sure the goddess"1.2.424)-- rejection of lame Caliban for "divine" Ferdinand ("a thing divine" (1.2.421), who is a Martian figure, whose game is the war game of chess: "Yes, for a score of kingdoms you should wrangle, / And I would call it fair play" (5.1.173-4).

4. Ariel's words "Hark, hark! I hear the strain of strutting chauntecleer" (1.2.387-8) are an allusion

to Mars' changing of the youth Alectryon into a rooster--the youth was set to warn Mars against the approach of Helios (the sun) during his rendezvous with Venus; the lad fell asleep and was punished by being transformed into a rooster, which now atones for his old fault by routine crowing at the sun's daily approach. The rooster reappears later:

Antonio: Which...first
begins to crow?
Sebastian: The old cock (2.1.26-28).

Minerva and Pandora vs. Miranda

Mother Earth (Gaia) abandoned Vulcan's son Erichthonius born off her, but Minerva took the infant, half-human and half-serpent, put him in a chest, and asked the daughters of Cecrops to guard it. The curiosity of the girls got the better of them, and they opened the chest. Upon seeing the serpent tail, they leaped to their death from the Acropolis. A white crow brought the sad news to Minerva, who changed the crow's color from white to black in anger and frustration and banished the crow from the Acropolis. Minerva herself later reared the child Erichthonius and made him king of Athens.

Vulcan made Pandora at the request of Jupiter for the purpose of punishing Prometheus who gave mankind the gift of fire, and all the gods made presents to her. Venus gave her beauty; Apollo taught her to sing; Minerva gave her splendid ornaments. In addition, Jupiter gave her a box as wedding present. When she (or her husband Epimetheus) opened the box, there issued from it a multitude of evils except for hope which remained at the bottom.

In the colonial discourse of popular imagination articulated by Mrs. Jameson, Miranda is a blend of pure nature and lofty ideal:

> We might have deemed it impossible to go beyond Viola, Perdita, and Ophelia as pictures of feminine beauty; to exceed the one in tender delicacy, the other in ideal grace, and the last in simplicity, if Shakespeare had not done this; and he alone could have done it. Had he never created a Miranda, we should never have been made to feel how completely the purely natural and the purely ideal can blend into each other.... She is beautiful, modest, and tender, and she is these only;.... She is so perfectly unsophisticated, so delicately refined, that she is all but ethereal.[19]

No doubt, Miranda has been all that in colonial imagination and colonial criticism, but in Shakespeare's carefully crafted post-colonial discourse she has another dimension, which is not at all flattering. I realize that the following discussion of the character of Miranda goes against all received interpretation of Miranda's character, but I argue that my reading of Miranda's multi-faceted character does make good sense against the mythological background of the play; therefore, a willing suspension of disbelief is a sine qua non at this point.

In her relationship to Caliban, Shakespeare portrays Mirand as a composite of Venus, Minerva, and Pandora. As a Venus-figure, as mentioned above, Miranda rejects the lame

Caliban in favor of Ferdinand.

Vulcan's attempt of ravishing Minerva parallels Caliban's reported attempt of embracing Miranda. However, a few unanswered questions remain: Did Prospero see Caliban's rape attempt? There is no textual evidence to support the position that Prospero actually saw Caliban's savage attack on Miranda, though Caliban does not deny the so-called rape charge: "..would't had been done!/ Thou didst prevent me " (1.1.351-2). It is one thing to think about having sex with/marrying someone and another thing to attempt it; Caliban does not admit that he tried to rape Miranda; he wished he had children with Miranda. If he wished he had children with Miranda, he thought that he was somehow married to her or that she was promised in marriage to him by Prospero. Of course, the text does not spell out all these ideas clearly. The "it" (1.2.351) could be interpreted as marriage in the mind of Caliban but unholy sex and miscegenation in the mind of Prospero, who by this time was having second thoughts about his vision of alliance between Miranda and Caliban. Did Miranda report "it" as attempted rape to Prospero? If the answer to the first question (Did Prospero see Caliban's attempted rape?) is negative or neutral, then the answer is that Prospero learned about the "marriage proposal"/rape attempt from Miranda (Sharp 267-83). Did the racially prejudiced Miranda interpret Caliban's speech of marriage proposal (?) to mean intention to rape?[20] The following of speech of Miranda shows her deep-rooted racial prejudices:

> Abhorred slave,
> Which any print of goodness wilt not take,
> Being capable of all ill? I pitied thee,
> Took pains to make thee speak, taught thee each hour
> One thing or other: when thou didst not, savage,
> Know thine own meaning, but wouldst gabble like
> A thing most brutish, I endow'd thy purposes
> With words that make them known. But thy vile race,
> Though thou didst learn, had that in't which good natures
> Could not abide to be with; therefore wast thou
> 'Deservedly confin'd into this rock (1.2.353-63).

This passage implies that Miranda was at least partially responsible for Caliban's education, just as Minerva was responsible for Erichthonius' and just as Thetis and Euronyme were for Vulcan's, and that, when Caliban was not able to express his thoughts, Miranda enabled him to make known what was on his mind: "I endow'd thy purposes with words that made them known (1.2.360). One could wonder how accurately Caliban could have expressed himself in a foreign language. However, Caliban's elegant use of the foreign language in the play seems to imply that he knew what he was talking about and that he was not an idiot. On the other hand, it seems Miranda reported to Prospero what she thought Caliban was thinking about and wanting to do. Miranda thought that Caliban wanted to possess her physically and she apparently reported it to Prospero who immediately took action by punishing Caliban. In other words, the colonialist Prospero got what he wanted to hear from the mouth of the so-called "victim" herself in order to punish Caliban according to his changed colonialist plans. Even if Prospero had intended to bestow Miranda on Caliban and promised that Caliban could marry her, without Miranda I can only say that she did not give her required consent to Prospero's marriage plans for her, as was probably the case of the marriage between Venus and Vulcan. Who would disbelieve Miranda?

Certainly, Caliban, who speaks in blank verse, must have learned this poetic speech from Miranda. Interestingly, he also learned to curse from Miranda: "You taught me language; and my profit on 't/Is, I know how to curse" (1.2.363-4).[22] If Caliban learned how to curse from Miranda, she certainly is not as holy and innocent, modest and tender, sophisticated and refined, truthful and sly as she is made out to be by colonial critics like Mrs. Jameson. However we interpret this passage, it's useful to remember that Shakespeare is deliberately obtuse not only about Caliban but also about Miranda. As Stephen Greenblatt reminds us, "Caliban's world has what we may call *opacity*, and perfect emblem of that opacity is the fact that we do not to this day know the meaning of the word, "scamel" [in I'll bring thee / To clustering filberts, and sometimes I'll get thee / Young scamels from the rock' (2.2.170-2) (31).[23]

In reality, if there was only a putative rape attempt or if the rape concept was only in the mind of Miranda, then Miranda brought misery into the life of Caliban by having him punished unjustly.[24] If that is the case, but for Miranda Caliban would have been loved and cherished by Prospero (?) just as Vulcan would have been loved and cherished by Jupiter but for Juno. It is in this sense that Miranda is like Pandora who, mythologically speaking, brought disaster on mankind. Like the curious Pandora, Miranda is "so perfect and so peerless...*created /Of every creature's best*" (italics mine--to indicate the creation story of Pandora who was given gifts by all the gods) (3.1.46-7). The Pandora of mythology could not repress her curiosity as to the contents of the box and she opened it unleashing a horde of evils on men. Miranda's denial that she is not curious-- "More to know/Did never meddle with my thoughts (1.2.23-4)--is a negative way of saying, "I want to know." According to the myth, Pandora opens the box and lets out all evils, leaving only hope behind. Shakespeare refers to boxes at least three times in the play: "What do you mean? / To dote on such luggage (4.1.230-1); "Bestow your luggage where you found it (5.1.298); "The ivy which had hid my princely trunk / And suck'd my verdure on't. Thou attend'st not?" (1.2.86-7). The last passage signifies loss of freshness, vigor, and power and the person to whom the passage is addressed is Miranda, who does not seem to be paying attention to her father's speech.[25]

It is noteworthy that the name *Miranda* means "to be marveled at" and that it is a blend of *Minerva* and *Pandora*. Additionally, when Pandora was brought into the presence of humans, they marveled at her as does Ferdinand when he sees Miranda: "Most sure the goddess" (1.2.424).[26]

Juno vs. Sycorax

Juno at first repulsed the advances of her crafty brother Jupiter. He beguiled her by assuming the form of a cuckoo and approached her on Mount Thomax. Juno picked up the bird and nestled it in her bosom. Immediately Jupiter resumed his original form and ravished her. When the arrogance of Jupiter became unbearable, the gods, under Juno's leadership, bound him in his sleep. Thetis and Briareus managed to free Jupiter, who, upon his release, seized Juno, the ringleader of the rebels and hung her out of heaven on anvils on her feet. Vulcan begged his father to pardon Juno.

Sycorax, the mother of Caliban, is like Juno, Vulcan's mother. The name *Sycorax* is derived from the Greek *sus* (sow) and *korax* (crow). Apart from Sycorax's possible association with the classical witch Circe who transformed men into pigs, Sycorax is a Juno-figure also on account of her connection to the raven, which was a sacred bird to Juno before the peacock took over (Avery 539). Shakespeare connects Sycorax with the raven in 1.2.323-4: "As wicked dew as e'er my mother brush'd / With raven's feather from unwholsome fen" (Kermode 30). Interestingly, "dew" means "fog" and "darkness" in Welsh, a language Shakespeare was probably familiar with. By associating Caliban with Corax, the raven, Shakespeare is alluding to the black color of

Caliban, the African skin color that Caliban inherits as a hamite/Chamite, as the son of Ham/Cham.

Jupiter-Setebos vs. Prospero

Jupiter, the husband of Juno, is the father of Vulcan, Mars, the Graces, Venus, and Minerva. He reigns on Mount Olympus as the Supreme God and wields the thuderbolt as his favorite weapon. Jupter not only controls gods and humans but also establishes law and order on earth, in heaven, and in hell.

Setebos, the god of Caliban, is supposedly one of the gods/devils of the Patagonians.[27] He could also be a classical allusion to Zeus who took the form of a bull (*bos*) when he carried off Europa. Also, the African Goddess Io was once transformed into a heffer by Zeus who tried to rescue her from the wrath of jealous Juno. Setebos with the Greek masculine ending could very well be a pun on *theosebeos* ("god-fearing"). The Shakespearean Setebos is, therefore, not altogether a pejorative word in the total context of *The Tempest*, except in the mind of colonial conquerors. Though Prospero is a playwright like Shakespeare, he is not necessarily to be identified with Shakespeare.

In several ways Prospero is rather a Jupiter-figure. He is powerful enough to call up storms, produce thunder, and control the elements (5.1.33-50). He at first treated Caliban well as though he were his own child ("This thing of darkness / I acknowledge mine" (5.1.275-6)--

Vulcan is also black ("As black as Vulcan in the smoke of war") in *Twelfth Night* 5.1.49)--and later punished him as Jupiter punished Vulcan for taking Juno's side. Prospero controlled Sycorax as Jove tried to control Juno, and he released Ariel from captivity as Jupiter delivered Ares from his prison. Thus, Prospero appears to be God-fearing or *theosebeos*; this aspect of Prospero has already received much attention from teachers and critics of *The Tempest*. So it is unnecessary to belabor the issue here.

The name Prospero contains the Latin word "spero," which means "I hope"; *pro* in Greek means "in the place of," as in prophet, who speaks in the place of God. Thus, Prospero is not only the beneficent one but also the personification of hope. If the story of Pandora suggests that there is always room for hope, Shakespeare indicates that it is the Prospero-like figure of King James I who is that source of hope: King James still can reverse the course of colonial history by freeing the colonized from serfdom just as Prospero released Ariel and Caliban from slavery. Further, King James could even allow intermarriage between the Europeans and the Indians as he had already approved the marriage of Pocahontas and John Rolfe.

Colonial Discourse

Kermode and other critics have already called attention to Shakespeare's awareness and use of contemporary colonial texts written by Strachey, Jourdain, and Florio. Kermode is probably correct in stating that Shakespeare has these documents in mind and that, "though they are of the greatest interest and usefulness, they are only of subsidiary interest and not fundamental to [the play's] structure of ideas." (xxv-xxxiv) It is for this reason that he prints these "sources" in an appendix to his edition. This editorial action seems to imply the New Critical assumption of isolating text from contexts; understandably New Historicists want to put them back together. While agreeing with both Kermode and the New Historicists, I believe critical strategy requires that we explore the relationship between the text and its subtexts. I have done just that by showing that the mythological subtexts, though relegated in received interpretation to the background, are central to the meaning of the play. On the other hand, though the colonial subtexts are in the foreground, Shakespeare cleverly embeds them in the mythological texture of the play.

The colonial subtexts are crucial to Shakespeare's (post-)colonial discourse. For example, Shakespeare suggests that colonialists are usurpers of lands that did not belong to them and enslavers of people who are free. When Caliban claims original sovreignty ("This island's mine, by Sycorax my mother / Which thou tak'st from me," (1.2.333-4), Prospero does not deny it directly by an emphatic NO. He rather replies evasively, "Thou most lying slave" (1.2.346) and goes on to accuse Caliban of attempted rape. Caliban tells Prospero, the colonial master:

> I am all the subjects that you have,
> Which first was mine own King: and here you sty me
> In this hard rock, whiles you do keep from me
> the rest o' the' island (1.2.343-6).

Shakespeare levels the two charges on colonialism only indirectly, knowing that it would not be politically correct to challenge publicly the official colonial policy of the English government (Barker and Hulme 199-201). Nonetheless, as Skura puts it aptly and correctly,

Shakespeare was the first to show one of *us* mistreating a native, the first to represent a native from the inside, the first to allow a native to complain on stage, and the first to make that New World encounter problematic enough to generate the current attention to the play (58).

Of course, Shakespeare could get away with an indirect attack on the English nation's colonial policy on the pretext that he "was in part describing something much closer to home--as was Jonson when he called the London brothel district 'the Bermudas' or as would Donne when he found his America, his 'new founde land,' in the arms of his mistress" (58).

Shakespeare acknowledges the conjunction of mythology and colonialism by referring to the widower Aeneas who was on his way to colonize Italy and to the widow Dido who had already colonized Africa (1.2.66-90) in the context of the marriage of the King's daughter Claribel to the King of Tunis (1.2.66-90). By means of the story of the abandoned colonial project in the Bermudas, Shakespeare seems to suggest two alternate answers to the colonial problem: (1) One way to address peacefully the problem of countries and colonies is by alliance through marriage. Naples and Milan are peacefully united through the marriage of Ferdinand and Miranda; Naples and Tunis are also at peace through the marriage of Claribel and the Tunisian king. Shakespeare seems to imply that Troy and Carthage could have been united through the marriage of the widower Aeneas and the widow Dido and thus have avoided the disastrous Punic wars. (2) If alliance through marriage is not feasible--as in the case of Miranda and Caliban--, the best way to deal with the natives of the colonies like Caliban and to make them friends is to give them freedom--as in the case of Ariel; otherwise, the natives and enemies of the colonists could always be a threat to the life and security of the colonial rulers, as the Trinculo-Stephano-Caliban plot indicates:

I had forgot that foul conspiracy
Of the beast Caliban and his confederates
Against my life: the minute of their plot
Is almost come (4.1.139-42).

Prospero's fear, apprehension, and anger are voiced by Ferdinand and Miranda:

Ferdinand: This is strange: your father's in some passion
That works him strongly.

Miranda: Never till this day
Saw I him touch'd with anger, so distemper'd
(4.1.143-5).

In post-colonial discourse, the story of
Caliban's "attempted rape" makes some sense: If
the natives are deprived of their land and made
into slaves, they might retaliate by raping the
colonial women while serving their powerful
masters out of fear (Caliban: "I must obey: his Art
is of such pow'r" (1.2.374)). Once Caliban is freed,
he is no longer a threat to the colonists: "I'll be
wise hereafter,/And seek for grace (5.1.294-5).
The idealist in Shakespeare seems to envision this
kind of a utopia:

> O, wonder!
> How many goodly creatures are there here!
> How beauteous mankind is! O brave new world!
> That has such people in it (5.1.182-4).
> The next minute, the realist in Shakespeare dismisses
> this ideal world as a dream:
> These our actors
> As I foretold you, were all spirits, and
> Are melted into air, into thin air:
> ....
> We are such stuff
> As dreams are made on (4.1.148-57).

It is possible to say that Miranda had a change
of mind as to her extremely negative view of the
"vile race" of Caliban, counted Caliban also
among the "goodly creatures," and incorporated
him into "beauteous mankind" at the end of the
play. Nonetheless it is safe also to infer that
Caliban was not after all a diabolical figure from

the beginning of the play except in the rationalizing imagination of the colonizers like Prospero who were trying to justify their policy of enslaving their colonial subjects. In other words, Caliban is deformed and morally evil only in the eyes of the colonial rulers, Prospero and Miranda and their associates, who, as the play unfolds, are shown to be in no way morally superior to Caliban.[28]

Reconstruction

In the process of deconstructing the received historico-colonial interpretation of the character of Caliban, I have tried to show the "other" dimension of *The Tempest* and reconstruct the play's a-historicist, mythological context, which is inhabited by spirits like Vulcan, Mars, Minerva, Venus, Pandora, Juno and Jupiter. By introducing the masque, Shakespeare himself shows his intention that the mythological subtext is integral to the total texture of the play. Shakespeare seems to subordinate the colonial subtexts to the mythological subtexts by suggesting that colonial propaganda transforms gods into devils and witches and brutes--Setebos into a devil, Sycorax into a witch, and Caliban into a beast--whereas these beings are noble gods. Shakespeare seems to suggest the following hypotheses: If the Columbus-like Prospero, Pandora-like Miranda, Mars-like Ferdinand, and Butler Trinculo could all be "divine" figures, why shouldn't the Vulcan-like Caliban, though deformed, be also called a god? If the "divine" Prospero could father the non-pareil Miranda, why couldn't the "divine" Caliban also father a non-pareil like Pocahontas or Thomas Rolfe, both of whom Shakespeare probably met during the performance of Ben Jonson's masque at the White hall on the twelfth night of 1616?[29] Why not establish peace between England and the colonies through the policy of live-and-let-live and/or by means of the policy of peaceful integration through interracial marriage and eschew the principle of conquest and liquidation?

Naturally, it is outrageously naive to argue for a one-to-one identification of the dramatic characters with their mythical counterparts. Caliban is Vulcan, of course; but he is also a Native American. Miranda is Minerva, Venus, and Pandora; but she is also a European woman in the colonies. In this work, as elsewhere, Shakespeare dances from one classical character to another, from mythology to anthropology, from Old Europe to the New World--back and forth, which is a testament to his profound knowledge of Greek and Roman mythology as is evident in all his works which abound in classical allusions. As Skura says, Shakespeare "was not merely reproducing a preexistent [colonial] discourse; he was also crossing it with other discourses, changing, enlarging, skewing, and questioning it. Our sense of *The Tempest*'s participation in 'colonialist discourse' should be flexible enough to take account of such crossings" (69). Shakespeare even seems to have anticipated the evolution of the process of colonialism and suggested, by clinging to hope left behind by Pandora, some means to deal with it; but historically speaking, as mercantile and business interests triumphed, Shakespeare, as a critic of colonial expansionism, turned out to be an ineffectual angel and *The Tempest* a voice in the wilderness, a storm in an ale mug.

Conclusion

Shakespeare uses *Caliban* as a pun, suggesting more than one meaning. *Caliban*, besides having the less obvious meanings of "son of darkness" and "son of Cain," has two major meanings. In the colonial discourse, the name is an anagram of *cannibal*; in anti-/post-colonial-mythological discourse, *Caliban* is an anagram of *Vulcan/Mulciber*. The key to the double meaning of Caliban lies in the simultaneous colonial-mythological contextualization of the play. We can read *The Tempest* as a colonial play or as an anti-colonial play or as both. Reading *Caliban* as a pun in the classroom can serve as a springboard also for fruitful discussions of the other names in the play--Ariel, Miranda, Sycorax, and Prospero-- in the play's mythological-anti-colonial context.

WORKS CITED

Alter, Thomas S. "Iroquois Cannibalism: Fact No Fiction." *Ethno-History* 27 (1980): 309-16.

Arens, W. *The Man-Eting Myth: Anthropology and Anthropophagy*. New York: Oxford UP, 1979.

Avery, Catherine B. *The New Century Classical Handbook*. New York: Appleton Century, 1962.

Barker, Francis and Peter Hulme. "Nymphs and Reapers Heavily Vanish: The Discursive Contexts of *The Tempest*." *Alternative Shakespeares*. Ed. John Drakakis. London: Methuen, 1985.

Bennet, Tony. "Text and History," in Peter Widdowson, ed. *Re-reading English*. London: Methuen, 1982.

Bernheimer, Richard. *The Wild Man in the Middle Ages*. Cambridge: Harvard UP, 1952.

Bhabha, Homi K. "The Other Question: Difference, discrimination, and the Discourse.," in Francis Barker, et al. *Literature, Politics and Theory*. London: Methuen, 1986.

Brown, Paul. "This Thing of Darkness I Acknowledge Mine": *The Tempest* and Discourse of Colonialism. " *Political Shakespeare: New Essays in*

Cultural Mterialism. Ithaca: Cornell UP, 1985. 48-71.

Cartelli, Thomas. "Prospero in Africa: The Tempest as Colonialist Text and Pretext." *Shakespeare Reproduced: The Text in History and Ideology*. Eds. Jean Howard and Marion O'Conner. London: Methuen, 1987. 99-115.

Chambers, E. K. *William Shakespeare: A Study of Facts and problems*. 2 vols. Oxford: Clarendon, 1930.

Erlich, Bruce. "Shakespeare's Colonial Metaphor: On the Social Function of Theatre in *The Tempest*." *Science and Society* 41 (1977): 43-65.

Fiedler, Leslie. *The Stranger in Shakespeare*. New York: Stein and Day. 1972.

Fleissner, Robert F. "Caliban's Name and 'Brave New World'," *Names* 40 (1992): 295-8.

Frye, Northrop. Ed. *The Tempest*. Baltimore: Penguin, 1971.

Goldsmith, Robert. "The Wild Man on the English Stage." *MLR* 53 (1958): 481-91.

Greenblatt, Stephen. "Learning to Curse: Aspects of Linguistic Colonialism in the Sixteenth Century." *First Images of America*. Ed. Fredi Chiappelli. 2 vols. Los Angeles: Univ. of California Press, 1976. 2: 561-80.

Greenblatt, Stephen. *Renaissance Self-Fashioning from More to Shakespeare*. Chicago: Univ. of Chicago

Press, 1980.

Griffiths, Trevor R. "This Island's Mine": Caliban and Colonialism." *Yearbook of English Studies* 13 (1983): 159-80.

Hamer, Michael. "The Ecological Basis for Aztec Sacrifice." *The American Ethnologist* 4 (1977): 117-35.

Hamilton, Donna B. *Virgil and the Tempest: The Politics of Imitation.* Columbus: Ohio State UP, 1990.

Harris, Marvin. *Cannibals and Kings: The Origins of Cultures.* New york: Random House, 1977.

Haskins, John E. "Caliban the Bestial Man." *PMLA* 62 (1947): 793-801.

Hirsch, E. D. *Validity in Interpretation.* New Haven: Yale UP, 1967.

Holland, Norman. "Caliban's Dream." *The Design Within: Psycho- Analytic Approaches to Shakespeare.* Ed. M. D. Faber. New York: Science House, 1970. 521-33.

Hulme, Peter. *Colonial Encounters: Europe and the native Caribbean,* 1492-1787. London: Methuen, 1986.

Hulme, Peter. "Hurricanes in the Caribbees: The Constitution of the Discourse of English Colonialism." *1642: Literature and Power in the Seventeenth Century.* Proceedings of the Essex Conference on the Sociology of Literature. Eds.

Francis Barker et al. Colchester: Univ. of Essex. 1981. 55-83.

Kermode, Frank. Ed. *The Tempest*. The Arden Shakespeare. 6th ed. Cambridge, Mass.: Harvard UP, 1958.

Las Casas, Bartolome de. *The Spanish Colonie*....Trans. M.M.S. London: 1583. Rpt. Amsterdam: Theatrum Orbis Terrarum. 1977.

Leininger, Lorie. "Cracking the Code of *The Tempest*." *Bucknell Review* 25 (1980): 354-59.

Montaigne, Michel de. *The Essayes of Montaigne*. Trans. John Florio. New York: The Modern Library, 1933.

Orgel, Stephen. Shakespeare and the Cannibals." *Cannibals, Witches, and Divorce: Estranging the Renaissance*. Ed. Marjorie Garber. Baltimore: Johns Hopkins UP. 1987. 40-66.

Orgel, Stephen. Ed. *The Tempest*. Oxford: Clarendon Press, 1987.

Sharp, Corona. "Caliban: The Primitive Man's Evolution." *Shakespeare Studies* 14 (1981): 267-83.

Skura, Meredith Anne. "Discourse and the Individual: The Case of Colonialism in *The Tempest*." *Shakespeare Quarterly* 40 (1989): 42-69.

The Tempest. Booklovers Edition. New York: The University Society, 1901.

Vaughn, Alden and Virginia Mason. *Shakespeare's*

Caliban: A Cultural History. Cambridge: Cambridge UP, 1991.

SHAKESPEARE NOTES

[1]As we shall see, Shakespeare's colonial discourse is very much akin to the spirit of contemporary post-colonial discourse. It is on account of Shakespeare's anticolonial spirit that I apply the term "post-colonial" to Shakespeare's discourse.

[2]Frank Kermode, ed. *The Tempest* (London: Methuen, 1961), 135-41. All quotations of the play are taken from this edition.

[3]Donna B. Hamilton, *Virgil and the Tempest: The Politics of Imitation* (Columbus: Ohio State University Press, 1990); Sandra Clark, *Shakespeare: The Tempest* (London: Penguin, 1980): 77-93.

[4]Paul A. Jorgensen, "Shakespeare's Brave New World," in Fredi Chiappelli et al., eds. *First Images of America: The Impact of the New World on the Old*; 2 vols. I (Berkeley: University of California Press, 1976): 83-90. *The Tempest*, ed. Morton Luce (first Arden edition), London: Methuen, 1901), pp. xxxii-xxxiv; *The Tempest*, ed. Frank Kermode, pp. xxxiii-xxx-ix, lxii-lxiii; *The Tempest*, ed. Stephen. Orgel, pp. 7-37; *The Tempest* (Pelican) ed. Northrop Frye (Baltimore: 1971), p. 15-24; Vaughan, p. 25

[5]Corona Sharp, "Caliban: The Primitive Man's Evolution," *Shakespeare Studies* 14 (1981): 267-83;

---

[1] As we shall see, Shakespeare's colonial discourse is very much akin to the spirit of contemporary post-colonial discourse. It is on account of Shakespeare's anti-colonial spirit that I apply the term post-colonial" to Shakespeare's discourse.

see also Bryan Crockett, " Calvin and Caliban: Naming the "Thing of Darkness," *The University of Dayton Review*, 21 (1991); 131-44.

[6]Homi K. Bhabha, "The other question: difference, discrimination and the discourse," in Francis Barker, et al., *Literature, Politics and Theory* (London: Methuen, 1986), p. 150: "The exercise of colonial power through discourse demands an articulation of forms of difference--racial and sexual. Such an articulation becomes crucial if it is held that the pleasure and desire and the economy of discourse, domination and power.... the epithets racial or sexual come to be seen as modes of differentiation, realized as multiple, cross-cutting determinations, polymorphous and perverse, always demanding a specific and strategic calculation of their effects."

[7]In *The Tempest*, physical deformity, sexual allegation and instruction of the native Caliban in Miranda's language play a major role (see below); see also Bruce Ehrlich, "Shakespeare's Colonial Metaphor: On the Social Function of Theatre in *The Tempest*," *Science and Society*, 41 (1977): 43-65.

[8]The clever friendly Indians told the colonists what they wanted to hear about their enemy Indians: They were man-eaters. The debate on this issue has been a lively one. See Michael Hamer, "The Ecological Basis for Aztec Sacrifice," *The American Ethnologist* 4 (1977): 117-35; Marvin Harris, *Cannibals and Kings: the Origins of Cultures* (New York: Random House, 1977); W. Arens, *The Man-Eating*

Myth: Anthropology and Anthropophagy (New York: Oxford, 1979); Thomas S. Alter, "Iroquois Cannibalism: Fact no Fiction," *Ethno-history* 27 (1980): 309-16.

[9] *The Plays of William Shakespeare...*, ed. Samuel Johnson and George Steevens (London: Bathhurst, 1778), I: 32

[10] Peter Hulme and Neil L. Whitehead, *Wild Majesty: Encounters with Caribs from Columbus to the Present Day* (Oxford: Clarendon, 1992), p. 3: "This schema has recently shown signs of collapsing under the weight of its own contradictions, not the least of which is that the language spoken by these "Island Caribs" was--and in the case of the Central American Black Caribs still is--a language affiliated to Arawakan rather than Cariban linguistic stock....The Old story of ferocious Caribs chasing timid Arawaks up the island chain from Venezuela, eating the men and possessing the women, is endlessly repeated in history primers and magazine articles, but fewer and fewer scholars will accept it. No new consensus has yet emerged, but recent work on the subtleties of cultural identity will ensure that any new version is more nuanced than the old, and less wedded to the stereotypes that served European colonialism so stalwartly." Admittedly the connection of the Caribs to anthropophagy was provided by Columbus's "Letter" of 1493, as transcribed by Las Casas: in January 1493, shortly, before his return to Europe, Columbus landed at a beach in

Española and he wrote about the natives he believed to be "of the Caribes who eat men" of whom he has heard (Hulme and Whitehead 27). Columbus was never certain about the cannibalism of the natives; Las Casas says that the admiral "believed that they may have captured some men and that, because they did not return to their own land, they would say that they were eaten" (*J* 69); cited by Peter Hulme, *Colonial Enclunters: Europe and the Native Caribbean, 1492-1797* (London: Methuen, 1986), p. 19)

[11]See Robert Fleissner, "Caliban's Name and 'Brave New World'," *Names* 40 (1992): 295-8.; Fleissner writes: "Columbus's locution of *cannibal* in some form derived from his misrepresented transcription of the name of the offending tribe as *caribs* or *canibs*, though the problem may actually have originated from the Taino tribe, ... or from Las Casas' own transcription of Columbus' daily journal of his first voyage" (296).

[12]In medieval and post-medieval exegesis, for example, in Alcuin, Cham/Ham, son of Noah, is confused with Cain. In the Noah story, Cham/Canan is destined to be servant Shem and Japheth (Genesis 9: 25); it is also important to note that Caliban is African in origin; according to Genesis 10:6, African nations are descendants of Cham; see also David Williams, *Cain and Beowulf: A Study in Secular Allegory* (Toronto: University of Toronto Press, 1982), pp. 16-17.

[13]John Reichert, "How Universal is the Bard?"

[the favorable review of the Vaughans' *Caliban*], *Amherst* (1992): 32, also asks: "Or was Shakespeare perhaps familiar with the Hindu word *kalee-ban* (a Hindu satyr)? Or the gypsy word *cauliban*, or blackness' (Prospero calls Caliban a 'thing of darkness')? Or was it *Kaleban*, an Arabic word for "vile dog'?" See Vaughan, p.33; E. K. Chambers, *William Shakespeare: A Study of Facts and Problems*, 2 vols., (Oxford: Clarendon, 1930), I: 494) said that "Caliban appears to be derived from the Gypsy *cauliban* "blackness."'

[14]Tony Bennet, "Text and History," in Peter Widdowson, ed., Re-reading English (London:; Methuen, 1982),p. 224.

[15]Francis Barker and Peter Hulme, "Nymphs and reapers vanish: the discursive con-texts of *The Tempest*," in John Frakakis, *Alternative Shakespeares* (London: Methuen, 1985), p. 193.

[16]Since Shakespeare uses the Roman gods in the play and the Roman Vulcan is identified with the Greek Hephaestus, I shall use the Roman names of the gods except Ares' throughout the paper, even though some of the myths deal with Vulcan are found only in the Greek texts like *The Iliad*.

[17]We have to bear in mind that, according to Shakespeare, Miranda is also a Venus figure in the play. The Venus of classical mythology rejects her husband Vulcan and dallies with Mars. It seems that Prospero at first out of sheer necessity tried to groom Caliban as Miranda's husband. It is likely

that there existed a promise of marriage (*consensus de futuro*) between Caliban and Miranda from Prospero's side, though there is no reason to believe that the marriage was consummated. On the other hand, later Miranda exchanges marriage consent with Ferdinand with a *consensus de praesenti* (3.1.83-89); legally speaking, present consent would take precedence over a previous future consent provided it was not ratified with consummation. Prospero has a change of plans after he discovers the Neapolitan prince Ferdinand on the sea and decides that Ferdindand would make a more suitable husband for Miranda than Caliban.

[18]Columbus's "Letter" (1493) mentions toward its end that he has found no monsters nor heard of any except on "una isla que es Carib," and which is Carib, and which becomes *Charis* ("Grace") or *Quaris* in the Latin editions. Is it possible that Shakespeare read Columbus's Letter in Latin?

[19]*The Tempest*, the Booklovers edition (New York: The University Society, 1901), p. 14.

[20]It seems that Miranda was also sexually repressed; the fact that the nubile Miranda was alone on the island seems to suggest that she was yearning for male company, and the fact that she falls for the first man (Ferdinand) she sees on the island invites Freudian interpretations of sexual repression.

[21]These lines are assigned in the play to Miranda. As Kermode comments, "Theobald followed

Dryden's guess, and gave these lines to Prospero; but none of the many editors has succeeded in justifying this interference" (32). The main arguments are that the language is too indelicate and too philosophical for Miranda and that she did not have much to do with Caliban's education and that she was too young on arrival in the island.

[22]This accusation of Caliban seems to be addressed to Miranda who berates him just before he speaks. In Greenblatt's reading, Caliban is "ugly, rude, and savage": "Caliban's retort might be taken as self-indictment: even with the gift of language his nature is so debased that he can only learn to curse. But the lines refuse to mean this; what we experience instead is a sense of their devastating justness. Ugly, rude, savage, Caliban nevertheless achieves for an instant an absolute if intolerably bitter moral victory" (*Learning to Curse* (New York: Routledge, 1992), p. 25.

[23]Robert Fleissner suggests that "scamels" is a pun on "mussels."

[24]The issue of Caliban's affections for Miranda may have some bearing on the Pocahontas story at least from the reader-response stance. In 1614, the Virginia planter John Rolfe who escaped unhurt from the Bermuda shipwreck wrote a letter seeking the Governor's blessing for his marriage with Pochontas, daughter of Powhatan--the colonizer wanting to marry a colonized woman who expresses "own inticements." This letter

indicates not just "unbridled desire of carnall affection: but for the good of this plantation, for the honour of our countrie, for the glory of God, for my own salvation." Already in the early 1900s Morton Luce had suggested that the published Pocahontas story of the young Native American Princess and Captain John Smith may underlie Shakespeare's account of the relationship between Miranda and Ferdinand ("Introduction" to the Arden edition of *The Tempest* (London, 1938), p. 169). Pocahontas' rescue of John Smith happened in December 1607, and John Smith's *A Trve Relation of such occurrences and accidents of noate as hath hapned in Virigina since the first planting of the Collony* was published in London in 1608 (*Works 1608-1631*, ed., Edward Arber, Birmingham, 1884, p. 38). John Smith calls Pocahontas "a child of tenne yeares old ... the only Non-pareil of his Country. This hee sent by his most trustie messenger, called Rawhunt, as much exceeding in deformitie of person; but of a subtill wit, and crafty vnderstanding" (Arber, p. 38). Peter Hulme points out that "Miranda is also a "non-parel" (III.ii.98) and Rawhunt suggests Caliban in his deformity and craft" (*Colonial Encounters: Europe and the native Caribbean, 1492-1797* (London: Methuen, 1986), p. 138). See also Warren M. Billings, ed. *The Old Dominion in the Seventeenth Century: A Documentary History of Virginia* (Chapel Hill: U of North Carolina Press, 1975), pp. 216-19; Grace Steele Woodward, *Pocahontas* (Norman: University of Oklahoma Press, 1969): 153-89; Paul Brown, "This thing of darkness I acknowledge mine": *The*

Tempest and the discourse of colonialism," in James Dollimore and Alan Sinfield, *Political Shakespeare: New Essays in Cultural Materialism*, (Ithaca: Cornell University Press, 1985), pp.48-71. I wonder whether Shakespeare incorporated the section on rape-charge in *The Tempest* after 1614 after he had become familiar with the story of John Rolfe and seen Pocahontas, who visited England in 1615. Geoffrey Bullough found the similarities between Miranda and Pocahontas so tantalizing that he called their identity "a tempting fancy which must be sternly repressed" (*Narrative and Dramatic Sources of Shakespeare*, VIII, 241; see Hulme, 137-73).

[25]Miranda-Pandora is also an Eve-figure, who, in traditional lore, did not pay attention to God's command not to eat of the fruit of the tree of the knowledge of good and evil in the Garden of Eden and who brought the punishment of expulsion from paradise for Adam and imposition of hard labor on him (as in the case of Caliban). The clue for this insight is found in

When thou cam'st first,

Thou stok'st me, and made much of me; wouldst give me

Water with berries in't; and teach me how

To name the bigger light, and how the less,

That burn by day and night: and then I lov'd thee (1.2.336-340), which is a reference to Genesis 1: 16, where the bigger light and lesser light are mentioned. If the context of this passage is Paradise, then Caliban is also an Adam-figure (implying potential husband-wife relationship with Miranda) with Prospero being a God-figure.

[26]Assuredly, the meeting of Ferdinand and Miranda carries an echo of Aeneas' meeting with his mother Venus in Carthage after his "shipwreck."

[27]According to Robert Eden, *History of Travailes* (1577), Magellan observes that the Patagonians "roared lyke bulls, and cryed upon theyr great devyll Setebos, to helpe them " (Kermode xxxii).

[28]In 1614, as he was dying, Shakespeare could afford to be more honest about his convictions and less afraid of truth and its consequences. More than likely, Shakespeare's anti-colonial discourse crept into the play only in its last version in 1614. Still by being indirect in his discourse and by using the parable of Caliban, Shakespeare might be echoing the Bible: "He who has ears, let him hear" (Matthew 13: 9 ff.).

[29]I realize that, in the absence of conclusive evidence, I am suggesting--just suggesting-- a later date for the present version of *The Tempest*. A later date for *The Tempest*, as it appears in the First Folio, makes much sense to me.

"The 'Divine' Caliban in Shakespeare's Postcolonial Dicourse: A Re(De)Construction," was first published in *Michigan Academician* XXX,399-422 (1998).

Final Conclusion

K. M. Pannikkar is right in stating that the 450 years, which began with arrival of Vasco da Gama in 1498 in Calicut and ended with the withdrawal of British forces from India in 1947 are marked by the domination of the peoples of Europe over the affairs of Asia.[145] It was during this period that India was "Orientalized"; or, as Edward Said puts it, "It can be argued that the major component in European culture is precisely what made that culture hegemonic both in and outside Europe: the idea of European identity as a superior one in comparison with all the non-European peoples and cultures. There is in addition the hegemony of European ideas about the Orient, themselves reiterating European superiority over Oriental backwardness."[146] However, this conception of European hegemony over India and the rest of the Orient as well as the superiority of the European vis-à-vis the inferiority of the Indian is the creation of the colonial mythographers. During the Classical and medieval periods the Indian enjoyed a high reputation as good, noble, civilized, and virtuous. The travel literature of early antiquity and the Middle Ages portrayed the Indians and their exemplary character as foils to European society and culture. On the other hand, the deterioration of the earlier myth began under missionary propaganda and its demise took place during colonial times with the simultaneous emergence of the myth of the savage   Indian.[147]

NOTES

1 See Jenny Sharpe, *Allegories of Empire: The Figure of Women in the Colonial Text.* (Minneapolis, 1993; see also Liz McMillen, "Post-Colonial Studies Plumb the Experiences of Living Under, and After, Imperialism," *Chronicle of Higher Education*," May 19, 1993: A6-A9.

2See McMillen, p. A 6. The classical example of this 2See McMillen, p. A 6. The classical example of this association of the uncivilized native attempting the rape of the Western woman is found in Shakespeare's *The Tempest,* where Caliban is accused of trying to rape Prospero's daughter Miranda.

3 The Tainos of the Arawak group, the first New World people Columbus met, greeted Columbus with hospitality and kindness.(see below).

4Samuel Eliot Morison, *Admiral of the Ocean Sea,* II (Boston, 1942): 168-177.

5Felipé Fernandez-Armesto, *Columbus* (Oxford, 1992): 103; F. Fernandez-Armesto, *Before Columbus* (Philadelphia, 1992): 230-235.

6Anthony Pagden, *European Encounters with the New World* (Yale, 1993): "For all Europeans, the events of October 1492 constituted a 'discovery'. Something of which they had had no prior knowledge had suddenly presented itself to their gaze. A 'New World' had now to be incorporated into their cosmographical, geographical and, ultimately, anthropological understanding. The term 'discovery--and its Romance analogues 'descubrimiento', 'scoperta', 'descobrimento', 'decouverte'--all derive from a late ecclesiastical Latin word 'disco-operio', meaning to uncover, to reveal, to expose to the gaze. It carries an implicit sense that what has now been revealed had an existence prior to and independent of the viewer" (5-6); see also Edmundo O'Gorman, *The Invention of America: An Inquiry into the Historical Nature of the New World and the Meaning of History* (Bloomington, 1961).

[7]Donald F. Lach, *Asia in the Making of Europe*, I (Chicago, 1965), 4.

[8]Stuart Piggot, *Prehistoric India to 1000 B.C.* (Harmondsworth, 1950), 207-208; cited by JeanSedlar, *India and the Greek World* (Totowa, 1980),3.

[9]Jean Sedlar, 5.

[10]Robert Caldwell, *A Comparative Grammar of the Dravidian or South-Indian Family of Languages* (London, 1913), 88-89; Max Müller, *The Science of Language* (New York, 1891), I: 188-191.

[11]Caldwell, 89.

[12]J. Kennedy, "The Early Commerce of Babylon with India," *JRAS* (1898), 252; J. Sayce, *Hibbert Lectures* (1887).

[13]H. G. Rawlinson, *Indian Historical Studies* (London, 1913),165-166.

[14]Sedlar, 5.

[15] See Zacharias P. Thundy, *Buddha and Christ: Nativity Stories and Indian Traditions* (Leiden, 1993), 212-217.

[16]E. Zeller, *Die Philosophie der Griechen in ihrer geschichtlichen*

Entwicklung, I (Darmstadt, 1963), 20; cited by Wilhelm Halbfass, *India and Europe* (Albany, 1988), 5.

[17]Halbfass, 5.

[18]Herodotus I.30.

[19]Diogenes Laërtius I.12; Halbfass, 6.

[20]Herodotus I.60 and Halbfass, 6.

[21]K. Karttunen, "The Reliability of the Indica of Ktesias," *Studia Orientalia* 50 (1981):105-107; Halbfass, 453.

[22]Halbfass, 11; W. Reese, *Die griechischen Nachrichten über Indien bis zum Feldzuge Alexanders des Grossen* (Leipzig, 1914), 66 ff.; Wecker, "India," *RE* 9 (1916): 1264-1325.

[23]C. A. Robinson, Jr. "The Extraordinary Ideas of Alexander the Great," *American Historical Review* 62 (1957): 326-327; L. Pearson, *The Lost Histories of Alexander the Great* (London, 1960); J. R. Hamilton, "Cleitarchus and Aristobolus," *Historia* 10 (1961): 448-458.

[24]E. H. Haight, *Essays on the Greek Romances* (New York, 1945).

[25]Tarn, *Alexander the Great* (Cambridge, 1948), I. ii: 145-146.

[26]Tarn,133, 233.

[27]Sedlar, 56-60.

[28]Lach, 10.

[29]James O. Thomson, *History of Ancient Geography* (New York, 1965), 158-167.

[30]Thomson, 135.

[31]Strabo,*Geography* II.3.3-5.

[32]Strabo, XV.1.4; Loeb VII.5; P. Thomas, "Roman Trade Centers on the Malabar Coast," *Indian Geographical Journal* 6 (1931-32): 230-240.

[33]M. P. Charlesworth, "Some Notes on the *Periplus Maris Erythraei*," *Classical Quarterly* (1928), 97.

[34]Lach, 14.

[35]*Periplus of the Erithraean Sea*, trans. Wilfred H. Schoff (New York, 1912); K.A. Nilakanta Sastri, *Foreign Notices of South India* (Madras, 1972); Sedlar, 91.

[36]Sastri, 57; Innes J. Miller, *The Spice Trade of the Roman Empire, 29 B.C to A.D. 641* (Oxford, 1969).

[37]Martin P. Charlesworth, "Roman Trade with India: A Resurvey," *Studies in Roman Economic and Social History in Honor of Allan Chester Johnson* (Princeton, 1951), 142; cited by Sedlar, 93.

[38]Karl Lokotsch, *Etymologisches Wörterbuch der europäschen Wörter orientalischen Ursprungs* (Heidelberg, 1927); R. Caldwell, *Dravidian Languages*, 89-91; Sedlar, 93.

[39]V. Kanakasabbhai Pillai, *The Tamils Eighteen Hundred Years Ago* (Madras, 1966), 16-38; Sedlar,93-94; A. M. Mundadan, *History of Christianity in India* I (Bangalore, 1984): 69.

[40]*Periplus* 60; Ptolemy, *Geography* I.14.

[41]Sedlar, 94.

[42]*India Abroad*, May 12, 1989, p.22.

[43]Sedlar, 94.

[44]Tacitus, *The Annals of Imperial Rome* III.53.

[45]*Natural History* XII.84.Alaric's demand that the Roman emperor pay him "three thousand pounds of pepper" as ransom of Rome seems to suggest that there was vigorous trade going on between Rome and India even in the fifth century, that is, even after the disastrous division of the empire in 364 (Rawlinson, 151).

[46]Philostratos, *Life of Apollonius*, III.16; Loeb I.263.

[47]*Life of Apollonius*, II.41; Loeb I.227.

[48]*Life of Apollonius* III.51; Loeb I.337.

[49]*Life* VIII.&; Loeb I.303-305.

[50]*Life* V.30; Loeb I.533.

[51]Lucian, *Toxaris* , 34.

[52]*Philo*, ed. F. H. Colson, Loeb Library IX.62-66; cited by Thomas Hahn, "The Indian Tradition in Western Medieval Intellectual History," *Viator* 9 (1978), 213-234.

[53]*Florida*, cited by Hahn, 216.

[54]Plutarch, *Life of Alexander* 8.65; Hahn, 216; see Sir Edward Bysshe, *Palladius de Gentibus Indiae* (London, 1665) for a collection of ancient texts.

[55]Sedlar, 200.

[56]Eunapius, "Life of Plotinos," in Kenneth S. Guthrie, ed.,

Plotinos, Complete Works (London, 1918), 7-8; Sedlar, 199.

[57]Eric Segelberg, "Ammonios Sakkas," *Zeitschrift für Kirchengeschichte* 50 (1941), 140-142; Sedlar, 201.

[58]Henri de Lubac, *Aspects of Buddhism*, trans. George Lamb (London, 1953); *La Rencontre du Bouddhisme et de l'Occident* (Paris, 1952); "Textes alexandrins et bouddhiques," *Revue desSciences Religieuses* 27 (1937): 336-351.

[59]Halbfass, 3. Wilhelm Halbfass assesses the worth of Diogenes' contributions:

Diogenes' reputation is that of a compiler; he presents and arranges his materials without any deeper understanding, and he does not provide philosophical perspectives of his own. His discussion of the origin and autonomy of Greek philosophy follows mostly older opinions. He neglects the "latest views" of his contemporaries in this matter. Neoplatonist, Neopythagorean, Jewish and Christian philosophers, who responded to this question with new intensity while presenting the relationship between Greek and Oriental culture in new and different perspectives and contexts, receive only slight attention in Diogenes' discussion. Diogenes is Hellenizing and "classicist" in approach. Further, in spite of his "compilatory" style, his personal position in the controversy with which he introduces his work is unambiguous: the origin of philosophy, in his view, is Greek, nothing but Greek. He goes on to state that the term "philosophy" itself defies all attempts at translation into Oriental, "barbaric" languages.(3); Diogenes Laërtius, *Lives of Eminent Philosophers* I.7; IX.61.

[60]M. R. James, "The Acts of Thomas," in *The Apocryphal New Testament* (Oxford, 1924); Leslie W. Brown, *The Indian Christians of St. Thomas* (Cambridge, 1956); Eugene Tisserant, *Eastern Christianity in India* (Bombay, 1957).

[61]Sedlar, 182.

[62]Eusebius, *Ecclesiastical History* V.9-10; Loeb I. 461-463; Sedlar, 180-181.

[63]*Stromateis* I.15; Patrologia Graeca (PG) 8.777; cited by A. J. Edmunds, 144.

[64]*Stromateis*, 3.7; PG 8:1164.

[65]*Stromateis* 4.7; PG 8.1263.

[66]The *Recognitiones* survive only in a Latin translation of the original; PG 1.1410; see Thomas Hahn, *art. cit.*.

[67]*Apologeticus* 42.1; Patrologia Latina (PL) 1.490-491:"Neque enim Brachmanae aut Indorum gymnosophistae sumus, silvicolae et exules vitae."

[68]Jean Filliozat, "La doctrine des Brahmanes d'après Saint Hippolyte," *Revue de l'histoire des religions* 130 (1945): 59-91.

[69]Prudentius, *Hamartigenia* 402-403; PL 59.1040.

[70]*De civitate Dei* 15.20; PL 41.463: "Et Indorum Gymnosophistae, qui nudi perhibentur philosophari in solitudinibus Indiae, cives ejus mundi sunt, et a generando se cohibent. Non est enim hoc bonum nisi cum fit secundum fidem summi boni, qui Deus est."

[71]Ambrose, *Epistola* 37; PL 16.1138.

[72]Sedlar, 168-170; Sir Charles, Eliot, *Hinduism and Buddhism* (New York, 1957), 423.

[73]Sedlar, 174; see Porphyry, *On Abstinence from Animal Food*, trans. John Dryden and A. H. Clough (Philadelphia, 1908), 171-172.

[74]Cited by Rawlinson, 225.

[75]H. G. Rawlinson, *Intercourse Between India and the Western World* (New York, 1971), 173.

[76]Rawlinson, 225; David Pingree, "Indian and Pseudo-Indian Passages in Greek and Latin Astronomical and Astrological Treatises," *Viator* 7 (1976): 142-195.

[77]Pingree, 144.

[78]Pingree, 142.

[79]Rawlinson, 226-227.

[80] Henri Pirenne, *Mohammed and Charlemagne*, trans. Bernard Miall (London, 1965), passim.

[81] André Wink, *Al Hind: The Making of the Indo-Islamic World* I (Leiden, 1991), 2-3.

[82]C. R. Beazley, *The Dawn of Modern Geography* (London, 1897):I: 98 ff.

[83] See Mabillon, *Acta Sanctorum Ordinis S. Benedicti*, . III, pars ii (Paris, 1672): 367-383

[84]Charles Plummer, *Two of the Saxon Chronicles Parallel* (Oxford, 1892): 79.

[85] See M. L. W. Laistner in A. P. Newton, *Travel and*

Travellers in the Middle Ages (New York, 1967), 32-33. It is uncertain whether these missionaries preached Christianity in India or Ethiopia.

86 A. M. Medlycott, *India and the Apostle St. Thomas* (London, 1905), 200; Mundadan, 118.

87 McCrindle, *The Christian Topography of Cosmas* (London,1897).

88See Laistner, 35.

89 K. A. Nilakanta Sastri, *Foreign Notices of South India from Megasthenes to Ma Huan* (Madras, 1972), 21.

90 J. Richard, "Les Missionaires Latins dans l'Inde au XIVe Siècle," *Studi Veneziani*, 12 (1970): 233; cited by Mundandan, 120.

91 M. N. Adler, ed. *The Itinerary of of Benjamin of Tudela* I(London, 1907), 63-64.

92Ibid, 65.

93 *The Travels of Marco Polo* , trans. Ronald Latham (New York, 1958), 265-266.

94 Ibid.

95 Ibid.

96 Ibid, 289-292.

97

https://en.wikipedia.org/wiki/Khajuraho_Group_of_Monuments: **The book is** "called *Taḥqīq mā li-l-hind min* *maqūlah maqbūlah fī al- ʿaql aw mardhūlah* (variously translated as "Verifying All That the Indians Recount, the Reasonable and the Unreasonable or "The book confirming what pertains to India, whether rational or despicable" in which he explored nearly every aspect of Indian life, including religion, history, geography, geology, science, and mathematics. During his journey through India, military and political histories were not of Al-Biruni's main focus. Instead, he decided to document the more civilian and scholarly areas of Hindu life such as culture, science, and religion."[97] Al Biruni had also translated the works of the Indian philosopher Patanjali with the title Tarjamat ketāb Bātanjalī fi'l-ḵalāṣ men al-ertebāk."

98

http://shunya.net/Pictures/NorthIndia/Khajuraho/Khajuraho.htm. The numerous reproductions of these erotic sculptures can be conveniently found on the Internet.

[99] https://en.wikipedia.org/wiki/Parvati

[100] Charles Nowell, "The Historical Prester John," *Speculum* 28 (1953): 435-445.

[101] See C. R. Beazley, *Dawn of Modern Geography*, III: 309-499.

[102] Yule and Cordier, *Cathay and the Way Thither* (Taipeh, 1966), III: 63-64..

103 Ibid.

104 See Beazley, III: 216-217. The martyred Italian Minorites came in the company of Friar Jordanus for the express purpose of preaching Christianity and converting Muslims and Hindus; see infra.

105 Yule and Cordier, II: 122ff.

106 Yule and Cordier,II: 178-179..

107Ibid, 267.

108 The four companions of Jordanus were killed by Muslims at Tana, and Jordanus recovered the relics with the help of a Genoese merchant and brought them to Supera from Tana; see Beazley, III: 217.

109See Beazley, III: 219.

110*Mirabilia descripta per fratrem Jordanum*, ed. M. Coquebert Montbret; Paris 1839: "Nomen nostrum Latinorum maius apud Indos, quam apud nos ipsos....Latinorum continue expectant adventum sive passagium, quia ferunt in ipsorum libris penitus esse scriptum...tota die rogant Dominum quod Latinorum acceleret optatum adventum"; See Beazley, III: 220.

111 Cited by Sastri, 214.

112 Yule and Cordier, II: 80.

113 Ibid.

114 See Beazley, III: 221.

115 Ibid. 226.

[116] Yule and Cordier, III: 212.

[117] Ibid. 254-256.

[118] Ibid 203.

[119] See Lynn White, jr., "Indic Elements in the Iconography of Petrarch's *Trionfo della Morte*," *Speculum* 49 (1974): 201-222; Ibid. "Tibet, India, Malaya as a Source of Western Technology," *American Historical Review* 65 (1960): 515-526.

[120] See Zacharias P. Thundy, *Buddha and Christ: Nativity Stories and Indian Religions* (Leiden, 1993); S. Radhakrishnan, *Eastern Religions and Western Thought* (Oxford, 1939).

[121] *Liber Cosmographicus* ; cited by A. P. Newton, 11.

[122] See G. G. Neill Wright, *The Writing of Arabic Numerals* (London, 1952): 37 ff.

[123] See D. J. A. Ross, *Alexander Historiatus* (London, 1963).

[124] Thomas Hahn, "The Indian Tradition in Western Medieval Intellectual History," *Viator* 9 (1978): 212-235.

[125] Peter Abelard, *Introductio ad theologiam* I: 22-23 (PL 178: 1032-33); *Theologia christiana* , 2 (PL 178: 1174).

[126] See Thomas Hahn, " The Indian Tradition" for more details.

[127] *The Travels of Sir John Mandeville*, trans. C. W. R. D. Mosley (New York, 1983), 178-80.

[128] Thomas Hahn, "Indians East and West:primitivism and savagery in English Discovery narratives of the sixteenth century," *The Journal of Medieval and Renaissance Studies*, 8

(1978): 77-114.

[129] *The Nature of the Four Elements*, Civ; cited by Hahn, p. 89.

[130]Ibid, C ii; Hahn, 90.

[131] *Epistolae* 3,4, and 6; cited by Hahn, 92.

[132] B. las Casas, *Historia de las Indias*, ed. A. Millares Carlo, 3 vols. (Mexico City, 1951); cited by Lyle N. McAlister, *Spain and Portugal in the New World 1492-1700* (Minneapolis, 1990), 84.

[133] *Cosmographiae introductio*, Gi and Diiii; cited by Hahn, 93.

[134] Ibid.

[135] *The Book of Duarte Barbosa*, trans. M. L. Dames, II (Madras, 1989): 34-37.

[136] *The Book of Duarte Barbosa*, I: 10.

[137] M. K. Kuriakose, *History of Christianity in India: Source Materials* (Madras, 1982), 30.

[138] "Xavier's Letter to the King of Portugal (1548)," Ibid., 37.

[139] "Francis Xavier's Letter of January 1545," Ibid., 33.

[140] See H. Taylor, *The Medieval Mind* (London, 1925), I: 332-335.

[141] The Bull Romanus Pontifex, January 8, 1455; F. G. Davenport, ed., *European Treaties Bearing on the History of the United States and Its Dependencies*, (Washington, D.C., 1917),I: 23; cited by Francis Jennings, Invasion of America (Chapel

Colonial India and the West

Hill, 1975), 4.

[142]The Bull Inter Caetera, May 3, 1493; Davenport, I: 61-63.

[143] James A. Williamson, ed., *The Cabot Voyages and Bristol Discovery under Henry II* (Cambridge, 1962), 49-53; 204-205; Jennings, 5.

[144] Quoted by Richard Ashcraft, "Leviathan Triumphant: Thomas Hobbes and the Politics of Wild Men," in *The Wild Man Within*, ed. E. Dudley and M. E. Novak (Pittsburgh, 1972), 151; see Hahn, 112.

[145] K. M. Pannikkar, *Asia and Western Dominance* (London, 1959), 13.

[146] Edward W. Said, *Orientalism* (New York, 1978), 7.

[147] I am grateful to the National Endowment for Humanities and John Carter Brown Library which gave me a grant in the summer of 1992 to attend the Early Maritime Studies Institute at Brown University. Part of the research for this paper was done during that summer at the John Carter Brown Library.

CPSIA information can be obtained
at www.ICGtesting.com
Printed in the USA
LVHW011910111222
735004LV00005B/630